# WORD ROOTS

## B2

### LEARNING THE BUILDING BLOCKS
### OF BETTER SPELLING AND VOCABULARY

**Word Roots Series**
📖 Beginning 📖 A1 📖 A2 📖 B1 📖 B2
Flashcards: Beginning • A1 • A2 • B1

Written by
## Cherie A. Plant

Graphic Design by
## Annette Langenstein

Edited by
## Patricia Gray
## Catherine Connors-Nelson

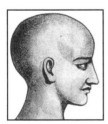

© 2011, 2005
THE CRITICAL THINKING CO.™
www.CriticalThinking.com
Phone: 800-458-4849 • Fax: 831-393-3277
P.O. Box 1610 • Seaside • CA 93955-1610
ISBN 978-0-89455-866-5

MIX
Paper from
responsible sources
FSC® C011935

# TABLE OF CONTENTS

# INTRODUCTION

". . . It is by means of words that one depicts his
feelings. It is therefore essential to one's success that
he be provided with a copious vocabulary."
—*Roget*

*Word Roots* is designed to help students expand their spelling, vocabulary, and comprehension skills. *Word Roots* is a uniquely designed and challenging workbook based on the word elements: roots, prefixes, and suffixes. Note that the roots used in this book originate from both the Greek and the Latin languages – the foundation of much of our English language.

Roots, prefixes, and suffixes are the building blocks upon which all words are formed. A thorough knowledge of these elements will greatly enhance one's vocabulary and improve one's understanding of otherwise unfamiliar words. For example, understanding the meaning of the roots **plac**, **trus**, **orth**, and **sequ** would enable one to comprehend numerous words made from combinations of these elements, such as the following:

| | | | |
|---|---|---|---|
| placate | intrusion | orthodox | obsequious |
| implacable | protrusive | orthotics | subsequent |
| placebo | unobtrusive | orthodontics | sequential |
| complacent | extrusion | orthopedist | non sequitur |

A single Greek or Latin root can be the basis for many words in the English language. The significance of this lies in the fact that with every new root learned, the resulting growth of one's vocabulary can be truly astounding – and *Word Roots* provides the tools.

## Definitions of Root, Prefix, and Suffix

A **root** is the element that gives the basic meaning of the word. In this book, the term root refers to the original Greek or Latin word. An English word may have two or more roots in it. Identifying these roots can help you to define a word you don't know.

A **prefix** is an element that is added to the beginning of a word. The prefix adds to or alters the meaning of the basic word. For example, the prefix **in-** means in, into. The root **flux** means flowing.

in + flux = influx  means the arrival of a large number of people or things

The prefix **re-** means back, again.

re + flux  = reflux means a backward flow

A **suffix** is an element added to the end of a word. The suffix modifies the meaning of the basic word.

Root: **magn** = great, large        Suffixes: **-ate** (one who), **-fy** (to do, to make), **-tude** (state, quality, act)

magn + ate = magnate means a person of high rank, power, influence, etc. in a specific field

magn + ify = magnify means to increase in size; enlarge

magn + itude = magnitude means greatness of size, volume, or extent

Words such as <u>af</u>flu<u>ence</u> and <u>ex</u>foli<u>ate</u> have both a prefix and a suffix joined to the root.

# How to Do the Activities

The worksheets help the student to meet several objectives.    Given Latin and Greek elements and their definitions, the student will:

1.  Identify these elements in English words.
2.  Match each given word to its correct meaning.
3.  Select the correct word to complete an unfinished sentence.

## Identifying the Elements

The information below will help the student identify the word elements (Objective 1 above).

*   A word can have more than one root, as shown below.   Each root is circled.

    thermo + meter  =   (thermo)(meter)

*   In some words, connecting vowels and/or consonants are used to join word parts or to complete a word.   For the sake of simplicity, connecting vowels and consonants used to join word parts or to complete words will appear in gray.

    herb + i +  cide = herbicide
    fer + t + ile = fertile
    medi + at + or = mediator
    de + scribe  =  describe

*   In some cases, to help smooth the sound of the spoken word, a vowel is added to a root.   This vowel (usually an o), is referred to as a <u>connecting vowel</u>, and the modified root is called a <u>combining form.</u>   For example, the root **hydr** uses the connecting vowel o to produce the combining form **hydro,** which then combines with the root **electr** and the suffix -**ic** to form the word **hydroelectric**. In the lessons, an asterisk (*) is used to indicate if a root is a combining form.

    hydr + o  =  hydro (combining form)
    hydro + electr + ic  = hydroelectric

Some roots are considered to be combining forms, yet do not follow the general rule.

*   The last letter may be dropped when a suffix is added.

    dermato + logy + ist    -**logy** drops the y in   (dermato)logist

*   Variations in the spelling of roots are given when necessary.   For example, some words include the root as **peps**, some as **pept**. The form of the root shown depends on the words used.   When both or all forms are used, the root is listed with its alternatives.   In some instances, an s is added to a suffix ending because the word is typically used in the plural form; for example, *repercussions*:  the effects, often indirect or remote, of some event or action.

## Completing the Exercises

Each worksheet is labelled with the focus elements for that page (see next page).   Each word in Column A includes at least one of the focus elements.   A 3-column box lists the word elements used on the page and their definitions.   A prefix *ends* with a hyphen ( - ) indicating that text follows; a suffix *begins* with a hyphen indicating that text precedes it.

The student should do each worksheet as instructed below:

1.  Study the meanings of the prefixes, roots, and suffixes given.

2. In Column A, identify the Greek and Latin elements used in each word by circling roots and underlining prefixes and suffixes.

3. For each word in Column A, write the letter of the correct meaning from Column B. For words taken from a specific subject, such as biology or botany, the subject is listed in parentheses after the definition.

4. Use the words from Column A to complete the sentences. Write or underline the best word to complete each sentence.

---

PARTIAL SAMPLE WORKSHEET

### FOCUS: surg, surrect (LATIN); traumat (GREEK)

| PREFIX | | ROOT | | SUFFIX | |
|---|---|---|---|---|---|
| in- | in, into; not | surg/ surrect | rise | -ic | like, related to |
| post- | after | traumat | shock, wound | -ion | an action or process; state, quality, act |

**DIRECTIONS:** In Column A, identify the elements in each word by circling roots and underlining prefixes and suffixes. Then match each word with its correct meaning from Column B.

COLUMN A                                         COLUMN B

1. in(surrec)ion          _b_          a. occurring as a result of or after injury

2. post-(traumat)ic       _a_          b. a rising up against established authority

**DIRECTIONS:** Choose the best word from Column A for each sentence. Use each word only once.

1. Following wartime combat, many veterans suffer from <u>post-traumatic</u> stress disorder.

2. The commandos planning the <u>insurrection</u> swore the participants to secrecy.

---

## Extension Worksheets

Extension activities, starting on page 62, can be used for assessment or additional practice. There are four extension activities for each group of exercises. Worksheets One, Two, Three, and Four review the words introduced on pages 1-15; Worksheets Five, Six, Seven, and Eight review pages 16 -30; Worksheets Nine, Ten, Eleven, and Twelve review pages 31-45; Worksheets Thirteen, Fourteen, Fifteen, and Sixteen review pages 46-61. Worksheet Seventeen includes words from the entire book.

# PRETEST/POSTTEST

 Before starting *Word Roots*, test your existing knowledge of word meanings. On the blank spaces provided, write what you think the following words mean. However, do not score your answers at this time. After you complete the book, take the test again, and then score your answers. Compare your answers from before and after to determine the progress you've made.

1. magnanimous _____

2. anemotropism _____

3. obsequious _____

4. ichthyofauna _____

5. selenosis _____

6. eucalyptus _____

7. tmesis _____

8. tumultuous _____

9. anechoic _____

10. ergonomics _____

11. exculpate _____

12. hypertrophy _____

13. glossolalia _____

14. oxymoron _____

15. amorphous _____

16. vermicelli _____

17. eolith _____

18. implacable _____

19. mnemonic _____

20. pendulous _____

# WARM-UP ACTIVITY: THINKING ABOUT MEANING

**DIRECTIONS**: Use the meanings of the given elements to define each word. The first has been done for you.

1.   **incombustible** = in + combust + ible ( prefix, root, suffix)
     **in-** means not; **combus** means burn up; **-ible** means able to be

     Then *incombustible* means <u>not capable of being burned</u>

2.   **mediation** = medi + ation (root, suffix)
     **medi** means middle, half; **-ation** means action, process

     Then *mediation* means _____

3.   **somnambulist** = somn + ambul + ist (root, root, suffix)
     **somn** means sleep; **ambul** means walk; **-ist** means one who

     Then *somnambulist* means _____

4.   **holocaust** = holo + caust (root, root)
     **holo** means entire, whole; **caust** means burn

     Then *holocaust* means _____

5.   **perturb** = per + turb (prefix, root)
     **per-** means through, very; **turb** means commotion, agitation

     Then *perturb* means _____

6.   **appendage** = ap + pend + age (prefix, root, suffix)
     **ap-** means to, toward, against; **pend** means hang, weigh; **-age** means state, quality, act

     Then *appendage* means _____

7.   **narcosynthesis** = narco + syn + thes + is (prefix, root, suffix)
     **narco-** means numbness, stupor; **syn** means with, together; **-thes** means to put, to place;
     **-is** means thing which

     Then *narcosynthesis* means _____

# FOCUS: acou, dog/dox

| PREFIX | | ROOT | | SUFFIX | |
|---|---|---|---|---|---|
| **para-** | beside, variation | **acou** | hear | st-**ic** | like, related to |
| | | **dog/ dox** | opinion, praise | **-ma** | something done |
| | | | | **-ology** | study of, science |
| | | **meter** | measure | | |
| | | **orth**o | straight, right | | |

**DIRECTIONS:** In Column A, identify the parts of each word by circling roots and then underlining prefixes and suffixes. Match each word to its correct meaning from Column B.

### COLUMN A

1. p a r a d o x     _____
2. a c o u s t i c     _____
3. d o g m a     _____
4. a c o u m e t e r     _____
5. d o x o l o g y     _____
6. o r t h o d o x     _____

### COLUMN B

a. adhering to what is commonly accepted
b. instrument which measures the acuteness of hearing (Physics)
c. related to hearing or to sound as it is heard
d. a liturgical formula of praise to God
e. a statement, situation, etc. that seems absurd or contradictory, but is or may be true
f. something held as an established opinion

**DIRECTIONS:** Choose the best word from Column A for each sentence. Use each word only once.

1. The conservatively run company hired him for his _____ views.

2. It is a _____ to Della that the harder she works, the less she seems to accomplish.

3. _____ is encountered in Jewish, Christian, and Islamic tradition.

4. The _____ apparatus of the human ear is amazingly intricate.

5. An _____ is used to test prospective airline pilots.

6. The political _____ of communism has always been oppressive.

# FOCUS: aesth/esth/esthesi/esthesio

| PREFIX | | ROOT | | SUFFIX | |
|---|---|---|---|---|---|
| **an-** | not, without | **aesth/** **esth/** **esthesi/** **esthesio** | feeling, perception, sensation | **-esia** | action, process |
| | | | | **-ete** | one who |
| | | | | **et-ic** | like, related to |
| | | **meter** | measure | **-ist** | one who |
| | | | | **-olog** | study of, science |

**DIRECTIONS:** In Column A, identify the parts of each word by circling roots and then underlining prefixes and suffixes. Match each word to its correct meaning from Column B.

### COLUMN A

1. a n e s t h e s i a     _____
2. a n e s t h e t i c     _____

3. e s t h e s i o m e t e r     _____
4. a e s t h e t e     _____
5. a n e s t h e s i o l o g i s t     _____

6. a e s t h e t i c     _____

### COLUMN B

a. an instrument used to measure tactile sensitivity
b. a doctor who specializes in administering drugs to prevent or relieve pain during surgery
c. relating to the enjoyment or study of beauty
d. a drug that causes temporary loss of bodily sensations
e. medically induced insensitivity to pain
f. one who has or affects artistic perception or appreciation of beauty

**DIRECTIONS:** Choose the best word from Column A for each sentence. Use each word only once.

1. The unsightliness of the post-war city would make an _____ shudder.

2. The new building has very little _____ appeal.

3. A less painful method of extracting teeth, called finger-pressure _____, has been developed by a medical school in Korea.

4. The _____ is the patient's advocate in the operating room.

5. With a local _____, the patient is awake during surgery.

6. One of the many uses for an _____ is to test children with afflictions such as cerebral palsy.

# FOCUS: agon, culp

| | PREFIX | | ROOT | | SUFFIX |
|---|---|---|---|---|---|
| **ant-** | against, opposite | **agon** | struggle | **-able** | able to be |
| **ex-** | out, away, from | **culp** | fault, blame | **-ate** | to make, to act; one who, that which |
| **in-** | in, into; not | **prot** | first, ahead | **-ic** | like, related to |
| | | | | **-ist** | one who |
| | | | | **-y** | state of, quality, act; body, group |

**DIRECTIONS:** In Column A, identify the parts of each word by circling roots and then underlining prefixes and suffixes. Match each word to its correct meaning from Column B.

### COLUMN A

1. e<u>x</u>(culp)<u>ate</u>         _____
2. a g o n y         _____
3. c u l p a b l e         _____
4. p r o t a g o n i s t         _____
5. a n t a g o n i s t i c         _____
6. i n c u l p a t e         _____

### COLUMN B

a. key figure in a contest or dispute; main character in a novel
b. contending with or opposing another; adversarial
c. to incriminate; to blame
d. deserving blame
e. an intense feeling of suffering
f. to clear from alleged fault or guilt; to free from blame

**DIRECTIONS:** Choose the best word from Column A for each sentence. Use each word only once.

1. His suspicious behavior tended to _____ him.

2. The attorney berated and was _____ toward the witnesses.

3. Despite the _____ from his shattered ankle, the athlete kept running.

4. Alex was confident that after the investigation, the court would _____ him of all charges.

5. The novel's _____ was characterized with the virtues of a classical hero.

6. The property owner was found guilty of _____ negligence in the accident involving an uncovered manhole.

# FOCUS: agora, fort

| PREFIX | | ROOT | | SUFFIX | |
|---|---|---|---|---|---|
| **com-** | with, together | **agora** | marketplace, assembly | **-able** | able to be |
| | | **fort** | strong | ific-**ation** | an action or process |
| | | **phob** | fear of | i-**fy** | to make, to act, to do |
| | | | | **-ia** | condition |
| | | | | i-**tude** | state, quality, act |

**DIRECTIONS:** In Column A, identify the parts of each word by circling roots and then underlining prefixes and suffixes. Match each word to its correct meaning from Column B.

### COLUMN A

1. (fort)itude          _____
2. agora          _____
3. fortification          _____
4. comfortable          _____
5. agoraphobia          _____
6. fortify          _____

### COLUMN B

a. an abnormal fear of being in open or public places
b. more than adequate
c. to strengthen, especially in order to protect
d. courage and strength in bearing pain or trouble
e. a gathering place
f. the act or process of strengthening

**DIRECTIONS:** Choose the best word from Column A for each sentence. Use each word only once.

1. Aunt Helen's _____ became obvious when she refused to leave her house.

2. Florida residents have to _____ their homes against hurricane damage.

3. Maurice showed remarkable _____ throughout his lengthy illness.

4. The sagging floor clearly needed stronger _____.

5. The _____ of ancient Greece was once the intellectual center of the world.

6. The candidate won the election by a _____ majority.

# FOCUS: anemo, bar/baro

| PREFIX | | ROOT | | SUFFIX | |
|---|---|---|---|---|---|
| **iso-** | equal | **anemo*** | wind | **-ic** | like, related to |
| | | **bar/** | pressure, weight | **-ism** | act, state, condition |
| | | **baro** | | **-logy** | study of, science |
| | | **meter/** | measure | **-ous** | having the quality of |
| | | **metr** | | | |
| | | **phil** | love, loving | | |
| | | **trop** | turn | | |

**DIRECTIONS:** In Column A, identify the parts of each word by circling roots and then underlining prefixes and suffixes. Match each word to its correct meaning from Column B.

### COLUMN A

1. barometric _____
2. anemometer _____
3. isobaric _____
4. anemophilous _____
5. anemotropism _____
6. barometer _____
7. anemology _____

### COLUMN B

a. pollinated by the wind
b. orientation in response to air currents
c. the study of the movements of the winds
d. related to or indicated by the barometer
e. an instrument for measuring atmospheric pressure
f. showing equal pressure
g. an instrument for measuring the force or speed of the wind; wind gauge

**DIRECTIONS:** Choose the best word from Column A for each sentence. Use each word only once.

1. In meteorology class, Mary learned how _____ helps to explain the effects of winds on the weather.

2. Honeybees and bumblebees actively gather _____ corn pollen, even though it has little nutritional value.

3. Wind velocity and _____ pressure are used to categorize the severity of a tornado.

4. The _____ indicated high winds; thus, forcing the ship to alter its course.

5. The _____ lines on the map showed calm weather patterns nationwide.

6. _____ occurs when hummingbirds poise for flight facing the wind.

7. The mercury _____ was invented by an Italian physicist in the 17th century.

*For more information, please refer to the Introduction.

# FOCUS: anth/antho

| PREFIX | ROOT | | SUFFIX | |
|--------|------|--|--------|--|
| | **anth/ antho** | flower | **-er** | one who, that which |
| | **chrys** | gold, yellow | **-ous** | having the quality of |
| | **graph** | write, written | **em-um** | of or belonging to |
| | **heli** | sun | **-us** | thing which |
| | **phag** | eat | **-y** | state of, quality, act; body, group |
| | **phyte** | plant | | |

**DIRECTIONS:** In Column A, identify the parts of each word by circling roots and then underlining prefixes and suffixes. Match each word to its correct meaning from Column B.

**COLUMN A**

1. anthography _____
2. anther _____
3. helianthus _____
4. anthophyte _____
5. chrysanthemum _____
6. anthophagous _____

**COLUMN B**

a. a flowering plant
b. any of a large group of plants with bright yellow, red, or white showy flowers that bloom in late summer or fall
c. description of flowers
d. the part of a flower that contains pollen
e. feeding on flowers
f. a group of tall yellow-flowered plants that include the sunflower

**DIRECTIONS:** Choose the best word from Column A for each sentence. Use each word only once.

1. The fruit of the potato plant is known to be a highly poisonous _____.

2. The _____ rootworm beetle is especially harmful to roses and chrysanthemums.

3. An _____ generally consists of two pollen sacs.

4. The _____ is the floral emblem of the imperial family of Japan.

5. The botanist gave an elaborate _____ of the over 200 species of chrysanthemums.

6. Some plants within the genus _____ are used to produce oil and birdseed.

# FOCUS: arch/archa/arche, hier/heiro

| PREFIX | ROOT | | SUFFIX | |
|---|---|---|---|---|
| | **arch/** **archa/** **arche** | first, chief, rule | **-ic** **-ics** **-y** | like, related to <br> science, system, related to <br> state of, quality, act; body, group |
| | **crac** | government, rule | | |
| | **glyph** | carve | | |
| | **hier/** **heiro** | sacred | | |
| | **type** | model, impression | | |

**DIRECTIONS:** In Column A, identify the parts of each word by circling roots and then underlining prefixes and suffixes. Match each word to its correct meaning from Column B.

### COLUMN A

1. archic         _____
2. hierocracy      _____
3. hierarch        _____
4. archetype       _____
5. hieroglyphics   _____
6. hierarchy       _____

### COLUMN B

a. the picture script of the ancient Egyptian priesthood
b. an original model on which something is patterned; prototype
c. a system in which people or things are arranged according to their rank or status
d. government by clergymen
e. belonging to an earlier period; ancient
f. a religious leader in a position of authority

**DIRECTIONS:** Choose the best word from Column A for each sentence. Use each word only once.

1. The famous novel I just read was the _____ of all other Civil War books.

2. He rose quickly through the political _____ to become party leader.

3. _____ were typically carved on the inner walls of tombs and on stone tablets.

4. Pope John Paul II was the reigning _____ of the Catholic Church for over twenty-five years.

5. Their government was based on _____ laws.

6. _____ prevailed throughout the Middle Ages.

# FOCUS: arct, thes/thet

| PREFIX | | ROOT | | SUFFIX | |
|---|---|---|---|---|---|
| **anti-** | against, opposite | **aort** | lift, raise | **-ate** | to make, to act; one who, that which |
| **co-** | with, together | **arct** | to press together | **-ation** | an action or process |
| **syn-** | with, together | **thes/ thet** | to place, to put | **-ia** | condition |
| | | | | **-ic** | like, related to |
| | | | | **-is** | thing which |
| | | | | **-ize** | to make, to act |

**DIRECTIONS:** In Column A, identify the parts of each word by circling roots and then underlining prefixes and suffixes. Match each word to its correct meaning from Column B.

**COLUMN A**

1. syn(thes)ize     _____
2. coarctate     _____
3. antithesis     _____
4. thesis     _____
5. aortarctia     _____
6. antithetic     _____
7. coarctation     _____

**COLUMN B**

a. a narrowing or constriction
b. directly contrasting or opposite
c. pressed together; closely connected
d. the exact opposite, contrast
e. combine so as to form a more complex product, etc.
f. the central idea in a piece of writing
g. narrowing of the aorta

**DIRECTIONS:** Choose the best word from Column A for each sentence. Use each word only once.

1. The _____ of his controversial book was that World War II could have been avoided.

2. The poem referred to the _____ symbolism of ice and flame.

3. His operas _____ music and drama in perfect harmony.

4. During the inactive stage of development some species of flies contain _____ pupae.

5. *A Tale of Two Cities* opens with the famous _____: "It was the best of times, it was the worst of times."

6. Although the best known _____ is of the aorta, it can appear in any artery.

7. The patient's _____ was corrected with angioplasty and the simultaneous placement of stints.

# FOCUS: asper, turb

| PREFIX | | ROOT | | SUFFIX | |
|---|---|---|---|---|---|
| **dis-** | apart, opposite of | **asper** | rough | **-ance** | state, quality, act |
| **ex-** | out, away, from | **turb** | commotion, agitation | **-ation** | an action or process |
| **per-** | through, very | | | ul-**ence** | state, quality, act |
| | | | | **-ine** | like, related to |
| | | | | id-**ity** | state, quality, act |

**DIRECTIONS:** In Column A, identify the parts of each word by circling roots and then underlining prefixes and suffixes. Match each word to its correct meaning from Column B.

### COLUMN A

1. ex(asper)ation  _____
2. turbulence  _____
3. asperity  _____

4. disturbance  _____
5. perturb  _____
6. turbidity  _____
7. turbine  _____

### COLUMN B

a. to disturb greatly; to upset
b. an interruption of a state of peace or quiet
c. a machine for producing power in which a wheel is made to revolve by a fast-moving flow of water, steam, gas, or air
d. a state of confusion and disorder
e. harshness or severity of manner or tone
f. annoyance and frustration
g. muddiness created by stirring up sediment or by having foreign particles suspended

**DIRECTIONS:** Choose the best word from Column A for each sentence. Use each word only once.

1. The Industrial Revolution was a period of great _____.

2. Residents were fed up with the _____ caused by the nightclub.

3. The girl feared that the news of her excessive truancy would _____ her parents.

4. Having fewer parts to malfunction, the rotary _____ engine has a distinct advantage over the piston type engine.

5. After ten hours of fruitless negotiations, he stormed out of the meeting in _____.

6. Their remarks, spoken with _____, stung the girls to whom they were directed.

7. The _____ of the water made it difficult to locate the fish.

# FOCUS: branchi/branchio, platy

| PREFIX | | ROOT | | SUFFIX | |
|---|---|---|---|---|---|
| **a-** | away, from; not, without | **branchi/ branchio** | gill | **-al** | like, related to; an action or process |
| | | **helminth** | worm | **-ate** | to make, to act; one who, that which |
| | | **platy*** | flat, broad | | |
| | | **pod/ pus** | foot | | |
| | | **rrhine** | nose | | |

**DIRECTIONS:** In Column A, identify the parts of each word by circling roots and then underlining prefixes and suffixes. Match each word to its correct meaning from Column B.

### COLUMN A

1. (branchi)al          _____

2. platypus          _____
3. abranchiate          _____
4. platyrrhine          _____
5. platyhelminth          _____
6. branchiopod          _____

### COLUMN B

a. parasitic or free-living worms having a flattened body
b. lacking gills
c. an aquatic animal with a broad, flat bill
d. of or relating to gills
e. characterized by a broad, flat nose
f. aquatic crustacean with gills on feet

**DIRECTIONS:** Choose the best word from Column A for each sentence. Use each word only once.

1. Fossils of _____ date back nearly 65 million years ago.

2. The duck-billed _____ is one of nature's most unusual creatures.

3. New World _____ monkeys are typically small, arboreal, and nocturnal.

4. The gills of fishes and amphibians are supported by a _____ arch of bone or cartilage.

5. The water flea is classified as a _____ and lives in water.

6. Salamanders develop into an _____ form as they mature.

*For more information, please refer to the Introduction.

# FOCUS: cant

| PREFIX | | ROOT | | SUFFIX | |
|---|---|---|---|---|---|
| **des-** | from, away, down, apart, not | **cant** | song | **-ation/** **ill-ation** | an action or process |
| **in-** | in, into; not | | | **i-cle** | small |
| **re-** | back, again | | | **a-trice** | feminine |

**DIRECTIONS:** In Column A, identify the parts of each word by circling roots and then underlining prefixes and suffixes. Match each word to its correct meaning from Column B.

### COLUMN A

1. in(can)tation _____
2. recant _____
3. cantillation _____
4. canticle _____
5. cantatrice _____
6. descant _____

### COLUMN B

a. the action of unaccompanied chanting in free rhythm
b. the chanting of supposedly magic words
c. high melody above the main melody
d. to withdraw something previously said
e. a hymn derived from the Bible; literally a "little" song
f. female professional singer

**DIRECTIONS:** Choose the best word from Column A for each sentence. Use each word only once.

1. The 'Magnificat' is a _____ taken from the New Testament.

2. In the Christmas concert, three members of the choir sang _____ while others sang bass and tenor.

3. They believed their _____ kept the evil spirits away.

4. He was forced to _____ his earlier statements about his religion.

5. _____ is typically part of Jewish liturgical ceremonies.

6. Barbara Strozzi, who published 125 pieces of vocal music in 17th century Italy, is often referred to as the most virtuosic_____.

# FOCUS: cephal/cephalo, morph

| PREFIX | | ROOT | | SUFFIX | |
|---|---|---|---|---|---|
| **a-** | away, from; not, without | **cephal/** **cephalo** | head, brain | **-ic** | like, related to |
| **di-** | two | **morph** | form | **-itis** | inflammation |
| **en-** | in, into | **thorax** | chest | **-ology** | study of, science |
| **meta-** | beyond, change | | | **-osis** | condition |
| | | | | **-ous** | having the quality of |

**DIRECTIONS:** In Column A, identify the parts of each word by circling roots and then underlining prefixes and suffixes. Match each word to its correct meaning from Column B.

**COLUMN A**

1. dimorphic _____
2. cephalic _____
3. morphology _____
4. metamorphosis _____
5. amorphous _____
6. encephalitis _____
7. cephalothorax _____

**COLUMN B**

a. a complete change of character, appearance, condition, etc.
b. the study of the form and structure of organisms
c. fused head and thorax of an arachnid or higher crustacean
d. without definite form; shapeless
e. of, or relating to the head
f. occurring or existing in two different forms
g. inflammation of the brain

**DIRECTIONS:** Choose the best word from Column A for each sentence. Use each word only once.

1. The _____ lab is analyzing the skeletal remains found during excavation.

2. The windstorm produced an _____ cloud of dust.

3. The Douglas fir is a _____ species of evergreen tree.

4. Muscular weakness, apathy, and profound lethargy are symptoms of _____.

5. Anthropologists use a special index in determining the _____ measurements of evolutionary man.

6. _____ is typical of all shrimp, lobsters, and crabs.

7. Brenda's _____ from a shy and awkward teenager to an accomplished journalist was quite impressive.

# FOCUS: cinct, cuss

| PREFIX | | ROOT | | SUFFIX | |
|---|---|---|---|---|---|
| con- | with, together | cinct | bind, border, surround | -ion/ | an action or process; state, quality, act |
| per- | through, very | cuss | strike, shake | -ions | |
| pre- | before | | | -ure | state, quality, act; that which; process, condition |
| re- | back, again | | | | |
| suc- | below, under | | | | |

**DIRECTIONS:** In Column A, identify the parts of each word by circling roots and then underlining prefixes and suffixes. Match each word to its correct meaning from Column B.

### COLUMN A

1. su(cinct)  _____

2. percussion  _____
3. cincture  _____
4. concussion  _____

5. precinct  _____

6. repercussions*  _____

### COLUMN B

a. an injury to the brain, often resulting from a blow to the head
b. anything that encircles, such as a belt or girdle
c. a part of a territory with definite bounds
d. the effects, often indirect or remote, of some event or action
e. the group of instruments that produces sound by being struck, such as drums, cymbals, and tambourines
f. expressed in few words; concise

**DIRECTIONS:** Choose the best word from Column A for each sentence. Use each word only once.

1. He suffered a mild _____ from the accident which left him dizzy and confused.

2. Elaine had to locate the right _____ where she would cast her ballot.

3. The novelist had a very _____ style of writing.

4. Jean plays the guitar in the band and her brother Vic is on _____.

5. War between two countries often has _____ throughout the world.

6. The _____ worn by the religious leader was bright red.

*Please refer to page iv, Identifying the Elements, for an explanation of why this word is plural.

# FOCUS: cinemat/cinemato/kin

| PREFIX | | ROOT | | SUFFIX | |
|---|---|---|---|---|---|
| **an-** | not, without | **cinemat/** **cinemato/** **kin** | motion | **iz-ation** | an action or process |
| | | | | **-esia** | action, process |
| | | | | **-esis** | action, process |
| | | **esth/** **esthe** | feeling, perception, sensation | **-ic/** **et-ic** | like, related to |
| | | | | **esi-ology** | study of, science |
| | | **graph** | write, written | **-y** | state of, quality, act; body group |

**DIRECTIONS:** In Column A, identify the parts of each word by circling roots and then underlining prefixes and suffixes. Match each word to its correct meaning from Column B.

**COLUMN A**

1. (kin)e_t_i_c_ _____
2. anesthekinesia _____
3. kinesthesis _____
4. cinematography _____
5. kinesiology _____
6. cinematization _____
7. cinematic _____

**COLUMN B**

a. the ability to feel movements of the limbs and body
b. the art and methods of photography used in film making
c. study of human musculoskeletal movement
d. the process of adapting a novel, play, etc. for film or movies
e. relating to the production or showing of motion pictures
f. related to movement
g. loss of sensibility and motor power

**DIRECTIONS:** Choose the best word from Column A for each sentence. Use each word only once.

1. The movie, *Lord of the Rings*, is a _____ of the trilogy written by J.R.R. Tolkien.

2. Today's interest in physical fitness and sports medicine has created many career opportunities in the field of _____.

3. The _____ effects in his films are clearly borrowed from the great film-makers of the past.

4. The Russian born sculptor, Naum Gabo, has many of his _____ works on display in London's Tate Gallery.

5. Ruth's spinal cord injury caused temporary _____.

6. *Citizen Kane* is an excellent example of superb _____ combined with creative use of sound.

7. _____ is very often stimulated by intense physical sports.

# FOCUS: ciner, combus

| PREFIX | ROOT | SUFFIX |
|---|---|---|
| **in-**    in, into; not | **ciner**    ash<br><br>**combus**    burn up | **-ary**    that which; someone or something that belongs to; of, related to; one who<br><br>**t-ible**    able to be<br><br>**at-or**    one who, that which; condition, state, activity<br><br>**-tion**    state, quality, act |

**DIRECTIONS:** In Column A, identify the parts of each word by circling roots and then underlining prefixes and suffixes. Match each word to its correct meaning from Column B.

### COLUMN A

1. in(combus)t<u>ible</u>  _____
2. cinerator  _____
3. combustion  _____
4. cinerary  _____
5. combustible  _____

### COLUMN B

a. act or process of burning
b. containing or used for ashes
c. able to burn easily
d. not capable of being burned
e. a furnace for burning waste under controlled conditions

**DIRECTIONS:** Choose the best word from Column A for each sentence. Use each word only once.

1. The small _____ formerly used in apartment houses has now been replaced by trash compactors.

2. The catacombs in the old cathedral contain vaults lined with recesses for _____ urns.

3. Due to its _____ nature, asbestos is used in the manufacture of iron safes.

4. The devastating car explosion was caused by the _____ gasoline vapors.

5. The fire which gutted the hops warehouse was most likely caused by spontaneous _____.

# FOCUS: colla, sphygm/sphygmo/sphyx

| PREFIX | | ROOT | | SUFFIX | |
|---|---|---|---|---|---|
| **a-** | away, from; not, without | **colla** | glue, gelatinous | **-age** | state, quality, act |
| | | **gen** | cause, birth, produce, race | **i-ation** | an action or process |
| | | **mano** | gas | **-ic** | like, related to |
| | | **meter** | measure | **-oid** | resembling |
| | | **sphygm/ sphygmo/ sphyx** | pulse | **-ous** | having the quality of |

**DIRECTIONS:** In Column A, identify the parts of each word by circling roots and then underlining prefixes and suffixes. Match each word to its correct meaning from Column B.

## COLUMN A

1. a(sphyx)iation   _____
2. collage   _____
3. sphygmic   _____
4. colloid   _____
5. sphygmomanometer   _____
6. collagenous   _____

## COLUMN B

a. a gelatinous substance
b. an instrument which measures blood pressure in the arteries
c. forming or producing collagen
d. an artistic composition made of various materials, such as paper, cloth, or wood, glued on a surface
e. act or process of causing suffocation
f. of or pertaining to the circulatory pulse

**DIRECTIONS:** Choose the best word from Column A for each sentence. Use each word only once.

1. The _____ indicated Clara's blood pressure was normal at 120/78.

2. A distinguishing property of a _____ is that its particles can scatter light.

3. _____ can be an extreme hazard when working in enclosed spaces, such as sewers or storage tanks.

4. _____ joint disease can be severe enough to simulate rheumatoid arthritis.

5. The nurse in the operating room monitored the patient's _____ changes throughout surgery.

6. The class used scraps of colorful material to make a Christmas_____.

# FOCUS: cryo, cryst

| PREFIX | ROOT | | SUFFIX | |
|---|---|---|---|---|
| | **cryo\*** | cold | **-ic** | like, related to |
| | **cryst** | crystal | **-ics** | science, related to, system |
| | **gen** | cause, birth, produce, race | all**-ine** | like, related to |
| | **phil** | love, loving | all**-ize** | to make, to act |
| | **scop** | look at, view, examine | **-y** | state of, quality, act; body, group |
| | **therap** | treatment | | |

**DIRECTIONS:** In Column A, identify the parts of each word by circling roots and then underlining prefixes and suffixes. Match each word to its correct meaning from Column B.

**COLUMN A**

1. (cry o)(phil)ic _____
2. crystalline _____
3. cryoscopy _____
4. crystallize _____
5. cryogenics _____
6. cryotherapy _____

**COLUMN B**

a. of the nature of crystals
b. the science dealing with the determination of the freezing points of liquids
c. cause to form crystals
d. capable of living at low temperatures
e. therapeutic use of cold
f. the science that deals with the production of extremely low temperatures (Physics)

**DIRECTIONS:** Choose the best word from Column A for each sentence. Use each word only once.

1. The _____ bacteria developed best at laboratory temperatures below 10 degrees C.

2. After centuries of pressure, a piece of coal can _____ and become a diamond.

3. _____ is currently used in such fields as space exploration, cattle development, food preservation, and surgery.

4. The surface of the lake had a _____ reflection when the sun hit it.

5. _____ has been very successful in permanently removing skin growths.

6. Chris was given a science assignment applying _____ with 12 different liquids.

# FOCUS: dactyl/dactylio/dactylo

| PREFIX | ROOT | | SUFFIX | |
|---|---|---|---|---|
| | **dactyl/** | finger, toe | **-logy** | study of, science |
| | **dactylio/** | | **-y** | state of, quality, act; body, group |
| | **dactylo** | | | |
| | **glyph** | carve | | |
| | **gram** | write, written | | |
| | **ptero** | wing, feather | | |
| | **scop** | look at, view, examine | | |
| | **zygo** | paired | | |

**DIRECTIONS:** In Column A, identify the parts of each word by circling roots and then underlining prefixes and suffixes. Match each word to its correct meaning from Column B.

**COLUMN A**

1. (dactylo)<u>logy</u>  _____
2. zygodactyl  _____
3. dactylogram  _____
4. dactylioglyph  _____
5. pterodactyl  _____
6. dactyloscopy  _____

**COLUMN B**

a. a fingerprint

b. the inscription of the engraver's name on a finger ring or gem

c. examination of fingerprints for purposes of identification

d. winged-fingered, prehistoric flying reptile

e. the science of communicating by using hand signs; sign language

f. having the toes arranged two in front and two behind

**DIRECTIONS:** Choose the best word from Column A for each sentence. Use each word only once.

1. Isabella was very proud of the _____ on her beautiful diamond tiara.

2. A _____ is a person's indelible mark.

3. _____ is one of the most invaluable tools used by crime fighters today.

4. As an aid to the hearing impaired, digital versions of _____ are widely available for computer keyboards.

5. Woodpeckers have _____ feet for climbing and perching vertically on the trunks of trees.

6. The _____ lived on lakeshores during the late Jurassic period.

# FOCUS: echo

| PREFIX | ROOT | SUFFIX |
|---|---|---|
| **an-**    not, without | **cardio**   heart<br>**echo**    sound<br>**gram**    write, written<br>**lal**     talk, babble<br>**locat**   place | **-ia**    condition<br>**-ic**    like, related to<br>**-ion**   an action or<br>       process; state,<br>       quality, act |

**DIRECTIONS:** In Column A, identify the parts of each word by circling roots and then underlining prefixes and suffixes. Match each word to its correct meaning from Column B.

### COLUMN A

1. echolocation  _____
2. echocardiogram  _____
3. echoic  _____
4. echolalia  _____
5. anechoic  _____

### COLUMN B

a. a means of locating an object using an emitted sound and the reflection back from it

b. involuntary parrot-like repetition of a word or phrase just spoken by another; echoing

c. free from echoes and reverberations

d. a noninvasive technique that uses ultrasound to record the functioning of the heart

e. formed in imitation of some natural sound

**DIRECTIONS:** Choose the best word from Column A for each sentence. Use each word only once.

1. Stereo systems are tested in _____ chambers which absorb all stray sounds.

2. Dolphins use _____ to navigate and find prey.

3. _____ is often seen in autistic children.

4. Advertisers make good use of _____ phrases like, "rice crispies snap, crackle, and pop," to help consumers remember their products.

5. Rosita's chest pains were so severe that an_____ was necessary for diagnosis.

# FOCUS: eo, lith/litho

| PREFIX | ROOT | | SUFFIX | |
|---|---|---|---|---|
| | **anthrop** | mankind, man | **-cene** | new, recent |
| | **eo** | dawn, early, | **-ic** | like, related to |
| | **graph** | write, written | **-us** | thing which |
| | **lith/** | stone | **-y** | state of, quality, act; body, group |
| | **litho** | | | |
| | **paleo*** | ancient, old | | |
| | **sphere** | ball | | |

**DIRECTIONS:** In Column A, identify the parts of each word by circling roots and then underlining prefixes and suffixes. Match each word to its correct meaning from Column B.

### COLUMN A

1. (litho)(sphere) _____
2. Paleolithic _____
3. Eoanthropus _____
4. eolith _____
5. lithography _____
6. Eocene _____

### COLUMN B

a. a genus of early man (comprising only the Piltdown man); dawn man
b. a very early and crude stone tool
c. the process or method of printing from a metal or stone surface
d. the outer part of the solid earth composed of rock
e. relating to the second epoch of the Tertiary period
f. related to the early Stone Age

**DIRECTIONS:** Choose the best word from Column A for each sentence. Use each word only once.

1. Geologists believe that the _____ was naturally formed and not of human design.

2. One typical style of _____ uses ink on a polished stone.

3. The stone implements characteristic of the _____ period were typically rough or chipped.

4. The discovery of the skull and jaw of _____ in England in 1908 was nothing more than a hoax.

5. The thickness of the _____ varies considerably from about one mile to approximately eighty miles.

6. Many modern species of birds first appeared in the _____ period.

# FOCUS: erg/ergo/urg

| PREFIX | ROOT | | SUFFIX | |
|---|---|---|---|---|
| **en-**  in, into | **erg/** **ergo/** **urg** | work, power | **-ia** | condition |
| | **gen** | cause, birth, race, produce | **-ic** | like, related to |
| | | | **-ics** | science, related to, system |
| | **metall** | metal, mine | **-ize** | to make, to act |
| | **meter** | measure | **-y** | state of, quality, act; body, group |
| | **nom** | name, law, custom, order | | |
| | **phob** | fear of | | |
| | **pyro*** | fire, heat | | |

**DIRECTIONS:** In Column A, identify the parts of each word by circling roots and then underlining prefixes and suffixes. Match each word to its correct meaning from Column B.

**COLUMN A**

1. ergometer         _____
2. metallurgy         _____
3. energize         _____
4. ergophobia         _____
5. pyrometallurgy         _____
6. ergonomics         _____
7. ergogenic         _____

**COLUMN B**

a. to make active
b. chemical metallurgy that depends on heat action
c. increasing capacity for physical or mental labor
d. a device for measuring work performance
e. the scientific design of products, machines, etc. to maximize user safety, comfort, and efficiency
f. the science and technology of extracting metals from their ores
g. abnormal and persistent fear of work or the workplace

**DIRECTIONS:** Choose the best word from Column A for each sentence. Use each word only once.

1. The candidate was actively campaigning in an attempt to _____ the voters.

2. The _____ of the new office furniture reduced eyestrain and back problems among the computer users.

3. Many sports figures have been known to use _____ drugs.

4. _____ of an ore involves roasting or smelting.

5. Most endurance-training machines today are equipped with an _____.

6. Saundra's _____ was brought on by anxiety over socializing with her co-workers.

7. Dana has a doctorate degree in _____ from the Colorado School of Mines.

# FOCUS: peps/pept

| PREFIX | | ROOT | | SUFFIX | |
|---|---|---|---|---|---|
| **dys-** | bad, badly | **calypt** | hidden, covered | **-ia** | condition |
| **eu-** | good, well | **peps/** | digest | **-ic** | like, related to |
| | | **pept** | | **-ide** | thing belonging to |
| | | **phor** | bear, produce | **-us** | thing which |

**DIRECTIONS:** In Column A, identify the parts of each word by circling roots and then underlining prefixes and suffixes. Match each word to its correct meaning from Column B.

### COLUMN A                                    COLUMN B

1. (pep)tic          _____     a. a feeling of great joy, excitement, or well-being, almost to the point of exaggeration
2. eucalyptus      _____     b. indigestion
3. dyspepsia       _____     c. relating to digestion
4. peptide           _____     d. good digestion
5. eupepsia        _____     e. Australian evergreen tree with rigid leaves and protected flowers and having medicinal and industrial value
6. euphoria        _____     f. a compound with amino bonds

**DIRECTIONS:** Choose the best word from Column A for each sentence. Use each word only once.

1. Eugene was in a state of _____ for weeks after he won the national championship.

2. _____ hydrolyzes into an amino acid and forms the basic building blocks of proteins.

3. _____ secretions exacerbated Janine's stomach ulcer.

4. The antacid relieved Matt's _____.

5. Betsy attributed her _____ to a healthy diet.

6. The oil from the _____ is a powerful natural disinfectant.

# FOCUS: felic, troph

| PREFIX | | ROOT | | SUFFIX | |
|---|---|---|---|---|---|
| **a-** | away, from; not, without | **felic** | pleasing, happy, suitable | **it-ation** | an action or process |
| **dys-** | bad, badly | **troph** | nourish | **-ic** | like, related to |
| **hyper-** | over, above | | | **-ity** | state, quality, act |
| **in-** | in, into; not | | | **it-ous** | having the quality of |
| | | | | **-y** | state of, quality, act; body group |

**DIRECTIONS:** In Column A, identify the parts of each word by circling roots and then underlining prefixes and suffixes. Match each word to its correct meaning from Column B.

**COLUMN A**

1. hyper(troph)y  _____

2. felicity  _____

3. atrophy  _____

4. infelicitous  _____

5. dystrophy  _____

6. felicitation  _____

7. trophic  _____

**COLUMN B**

a. to waste away or to decrease in size (as of a body part or tissue)

b. of or relating to nutrition

c. any degenerative disorder resulting from inadequate or faulty nutrition

d. an expression of pleasure at the success or good fortune of another

e. unsuitable; inappropriate

f. pleasing and appropriate manner; happiness

g. excessive growth or enlargement of a body part or organ

**DIRECTIONS:** Choose the best word from Column A for each sentence. Use each word only once.

1. As a songwriter, William has the knack for combining great linguistic _____ with an ear for a tune.

2. Many athletes experience _____ of muscle cells as a result of increased exercise.

3. Having to be in a cast for five months, Eric fears his leg muscles will _____.

4. His article was full of erroneous and _____ remarks.

5. Her muscles showed a marked _____, which made walking difficult.

6. The guest offered a _____ to the engaged couple.

7. The captives were poorly fed and suffering from _____ disorders.

# FOCUS: flu/fluc/flux

| PREFIX | | ROOT | | SUFFIX | |
|---|---|---|---|---|---|
| **af-** | to, toward, against | **flu/** | flowing | **i-al** | like, related to; an action or process |
| **ef-** | out | **fluc/** | | **tu-ation** | an action or process |
| **in-** | in, into; not | **flux** | | **-ence/** | state, quality, act |
| **re-** | back, again | | | **-ency** | |
| | | | | **-ent** | one who, that which; like, related to |

**DIRECTIONS:** In Column A, identify the parts of each word by circling roots and then underlining prefixes and suffixes. Match each word to its correct meaning from Column B.

### COLUMN A

1. af(flu)ence _____
2. fluctuation _____
3. fluency _____
4. influential _____
5. influx _____
6. reflux _____
7. effluent _____

### COLUMN B

a. variation in level, degree; constant change
b. an abundance of material wealth
c. a backward flow
d. the arrival of a large number of people or things
e. effortless expression
f. having a great deal of power to change something
g. flowing outward or forward

**DIRECTIONS:** Choose the best word from Column A for each sentence. Use each word only once.

1. Curbing the _____ of illegal immigrants is an ongoing task for border patrol.

2. The _____ stream originated from the highway drainage ditches.

3. Signs of _____ abounded throughout the neighborhood.

4. _____ in the price of fresh produce is highly seasonal.

5. Haley became an _____ CEO within the corporation.

6. Raymond's _____ in speaking five languages got him the job of interpreter.

7. His heartburn was due to acid _____.

# FOCUS: foli, somn

| PREFIX | | ROOT | | SUFFIX | |
|---|---|---|---|---|---|
| **ex-** | out, away, from | **ambul** | walk | **i-ac** | one who; related to, pertaining to |
| **in-** | in, into; not | **foli** | leaf | **-age** | state, quality, act |
| | | **somn** | sleep | **-ate** | to make, to act; one who, that which |
| | | | | **i-ferous** | producing |
| | | | | **-ist** | one who |
| | | | | **-ose** | having the quality of, a carbohydrate |

**DIRECTIONS:** In Column A, identify the parts of each word by circling roots and then underlining prefixes and suffixes. Match each word to its correct meaning from Column B.

### COLUMN A

1. (somn)(ambul)ist  _____
2. foliose  _____
3. somniferous  _____
4. exfoliate  _____
5. insomniac  _____
6. foliage  _____

### COLUMN B

a. person who is unable to sleep
b. to flake or peel off
c. leaves, as of a plant or tree
d. sleepwalker
e. covered with leaves; leafy
f. sleep inducing

**DIRECTIONS:** Choose the best word from Column A for each sentence. Use each word only once.

1. Being an _____ left Randy feeling tired all the time.

2. Brandi used a special cream to _____ old skin cells from her face.

3. The jarring sound of the door being unlocked snapped the _____ out of a deep trance.

4. The plant was so _____, one couldn't see light through it.

5. The poem was about a tree adorned with such exquisite _____.

6. A glass of warm milk at bedtime is reputed to have a _____ effect.

# FOCUS: glac

| PREFIX | | ROOT | | SUFFIX | |
|---|---|---|---|---|---|
| **de-** | from, away, down, apart, not | **fluvio** | flow | **i-al** | like, related to; an action or process |
| | | **glac** | ice | **i-arium** | place where |
| | | | | **i-ation** | an action or process |
| | | | | **-ier** | that which |
| | | | | **-ist** | one who |
| | | | | **i-olog/** | study of, science |
| | | | | **i-ology** | |

**DIRECTIONS:** In Column A, identify the parts of each word by circling roots and then underlining prefixes and suffixes. Match each word to its correct meaning from Column B.

**COLUMN A**

1. (glac)<u>iarium</u>      _____
2. glaciology      _____
3. deglaciation      _____
4. glacier      _____
5. fluvioglacial      _____
6. glaciologist      _____
7. glaciation      _____

**COLUMN B**

a. a slow moving mass of ice
b. expert in the formation, movements, etc. of glaciers
c. pertaining to streams flowing from glaciers or to the deposits made by such streams (Geology)
d. a skating rink with a floor of artificial ice
e. the process of being covered or covering with masses of ice
f. the scientific study of the nature, formation, and movement of glaciers
g. the gradual melting away of a glacier from the surface of a landmass

**DIRECTIONS:** Choose the best word from Column A for each sentence. Use each word only once.

1. A _____ that is bluish-emerald green in color signifies bacteria and other microbes living in the ice.

2. The _____ lectured on two general categories of _____: alpine and continental.

3. The world's first known _____ was opened in 1876 in London and was used solely by the noble of society.

4. During times of _____, supplies of _____ deposits often exceed a river's capacity, resulting in extensive sediment accumulation.

5. Unsurprisingly, _____ is one of the key areas supported by polar research.

# FOCUS: gloss/glosso/glot/glott

| PREFIX | | ROOT | | SUFFIX | |
|---|---|---|---|---|---|
| **epi-** | on, outside | **gloss/ glosso/ glot/ glott** | language, tongue | **-ary** | that which; someone or something that belongs to; of, related to; one who |
| | | **lal** | talk, babble | **-ia** | condition |
| | | **poly\*** | many | **-is** | thing which |
| | | | | **-itis** | inflammation |

**DIRECTIONS:** In Column A, identify the parts of each word by circling roots and then underlining prefixes and suffixes. Match each word to its correct meaning from Column B.

### COLUMN A

1. (poly)(glot) _____
2. glossary _____
3. glossitis _____
4. epiglottis _____
5. glossolalia _____

### COLUMN B

a. an alphabetical list of specialized words with their definitions, usually at the back of a book
b. repetitive non-meaningful speech
c. a person who speaks several different languages
d. inflammation of the tongue
e. a small flap at the back of the tongue that covers the windpipe during swallowing

**DIRECTIONS:** Choose the best word from Column A for each sentence. Use each word only once.

1. There was no reasonable explanation for Jessica's _____ while under hypnosis.

2. Being a _____, Tony had no problem while visiting many different countries.

3. The technical _____ contained only words which applied to PCB design and manufacturing.

4. Without an _____, a person would cough or choke every time he tried to eat.

5. Good oral hygiene, consisting of daily brushing and flossing, along with regular dental exams, may help prevent _____.

# FOCUS: greg, tum/tumori

| PREFIX | | ROOT | | SUFFIX | |
|---|---|---|---|---|---|
| **con-** | with, together | **gen** | cause, birth, race, produce | **-acious** | having the quality of |
| **se-** | apart, aside | | | **-arious** | of, related to |
| | | **greg** | herd, flock | **-ate** | to make, to act; one who, that which |
| | | **tum/** | swell | **-ation** | an action or process |
| | | **tum**ori | | **-escence** | growing |
| | | | | **-ic** | like, related to |
| | | | | ult**-uous** | having the quality of |

**DIRECTIONS:** In Column A, identify the parts of each word by circling roots and then underlining prefixes and suffixes. Match each word to its correct meaning from Column B.

### COLUMN A

1. (tum)ult<u>uous</u>  _____
2. congregation  _____
3. gregarious  _____
4. segregate  _____
5. tumorigenic  _____
6. contumacious  _____
7. tumescence  _____

### COLUMN B

a. producing or tending to produce tumors
b. willfully obstinate
c. full of commotion and uproar
d. condition of being swollen or enlarged
e. to set apart from the rest or from each other
f. a group of people or things gathered together; gathering
g. fond of company; sociable

**DIRECTIONS:** Choose the best word from Column A for each sentence. Use each word only once.

1. Fruit growers must _____ the good fruit from those that are bruised or blemished before going to market.

2. A _____ witness is subject to punishment.

3. His administration was marked by _____ years.

4. Unlike her twin sister, Lucille is outgoing and _____.

5. Ruben's head injury resulted in the _____ of brain tissue.

6. A _____ of news reporters waited outside the courtroom.

7. Cigarette smoking is known to have a _____ effect on lung tissue.

# FOCUS: hol/holo, stas/stat/statis

| PREFIX | ROOT | | SUFFIX | |
|---|---|---|---|---|
| **ec-**   out | **caust** | burn | **-ary** | that which; someone or something that belongs to; of, related to; one who |
| | **gram** | write, written | ist**-ic** | like, related to |
| | **hol/** | entire, whole | t**-ics** | science, related to, system |
| | **holo** | | **-ion** | an action or process; state, quality, act |
| | **stas/** | standing still | | |
| | **stat/** | | **-y** | state of, quality, act; body, group |
| | **statis** | | | |

**DIRECTIONS:** In Column A, identify the parts of each word by circling roots and then underlining prefixes and suffixes. Match each word to its correct meaning from Column B.

### COLUMN A

1. (stat)ion a r y _____
2. h o l o g r a m _____
3. h o l o c a u s t _____
4. s t a t i s t i c s _____
5. e c s t a s y _____
6. h o l i s t i c _____

### COLUMN B

a. a state beyond reason and self-control; overwhelming emotion
b. a collection of numerical data, facts
c. fixed in position
d. 3-dimensional photographical image
e. involving all of something
f. total or mass destruction

**DIRECTIONS:** Choose the best word from Column A for each sentence. Use each word only once.

1. As the money flowed out of the slot machine, his demeanor was one of _____.

2. The elderly woman used a _____ bicycle in her home to exercise.

3. They used _____ from several sources to determine which medicine was most effective.

4. When teaching reading, the professor preferred a _____ approach.

5. Children were shown, then asked to identify, the _____ of a famous person.

6. During World War II, the destruction of Jewish villages and the slaughter of their inhabitants was considered to be a _____.

# FOCUS: hypn/hypno

| PREFIX | ROOT | | SUFFIX | |
|--------|------|--|--------|--|
| | **hypn/** | sleep | **-ia** | condition |
| | **hypno*** | | **t-ic** | like, related to |
| | **narco*** | numbness, stupor | **t-ist** | one who |
| | **phob** | fear of | **-osis** | condition |
| | **therap** | treatment | **-y** | state of, quality, act; body, group |

**DIRECTIONS:** In Column A, identify the parts of each word by circling roots and then underlining prefixes and suffixes. Match each word to its correct meaning from Column B.

**COLUMN A**

1. (hypn)o_t__ist_ _____
2. hypnotherapy _____
3. hypnosis _____
4. narcohypnia _____
5. hypnotic _____
6. hypnophobia _____

**COLUMN B**

a. numbness experienced upon awakening
b. a state that resembles sleep but is induced by suggestion
c. an abnormal fear of falling asleep
d. the use of hypnosis in treating illness or emotional problems
e. a person who uses hypnosis as a form of treatment
f. relating to or involving sleep or hypnosis

**DIRECTIONS:** Choose the best word from Column A for each sentence. Use each word only once.

1. They were comforted by the _____ rhythm of the waves.

2. Kelly's nightmares were so terrifying that she developed _____.

3. Marlene went to a _____ to try to give up smoking.

4. Under deep _____ he remembered the traumatic events of the accident.

5. Mike's recent back injury caused him to have numerous episodes of _____.

6. _____ is sometimes used as a remedy for various phobias.

# FOCUS: ichthy/ichthyo

| PREFIX | ROOT | | SUFFIX | |
|---|---|---|---|---|
| | **fauna** | animal life | **-lite** | stone |
| | **ichthy/** | fish | **-logy** | study of, science |
| | **ichthyo** | | **-osis** | condition |
| | **saur** | lizard | | |

**DIRECTIONS:** In Column A, identify the parts of each word by circling roots and then underlining prefixes and suffixes. Match each word to its correct meaning from Column B.

| COLUMN A | COLUMN B |
|---|---|
| 1. (ichthy)o<u>lite</u> _____ | a. an extinct variety of fishlike marine reptiles of the Mesozoic period |
| 2. ichthyosis _____ | b. the fish of a particular region |
| 3. ichthyology _____ | c. the study of fishes |
| 4. ichthyosaur _____ | d. congenital disease in which the skin is fishlike (dry and scaly)(Medical) |
| 5. ichthyofauna _____ | e. a fossil fish or fragment of a fish |

**DIRECTIONS:** Choose the best word from Column A for each sentence. Use each word only once.

1. Bernice developed an interest in_____ when she lived in Australia off the Great Barrier Reef.

2. The _____ of the King George Island in Antarctica is highly exploited by commercial fishermen.

3. He cracked open the stone to find the withered form of a small _____.

4. Mike suffered from a chronic form of _____ that only affects males.

5. Fossil remains of the _____ have been found on every continent except Africa.

# FOCUS: lav/lu/luge, pur/purg/purge

| PREFIX | | ROOT | | SUFFIX | |
|---|---|---|---|---|---|
| **ab-** | away, from | **lav/** | wash, bathe | **-ate** | to make, to act; one who, that which |
| **de-** | from, away, down, apart, not | **lu/** | | | |
| | | **luge** | | **-ity** | state, quality, act |
| **di-** | apart, away, not | **pur/** | clean | **at-ory** | place where |
| **ex-** | out, away, from | **purg/** | | **-tion** | state, quality, act |
| | | **purge** | | | |

**DIRECTIONS:** In Column A, identify the parts of each word by circling roots and then underlining prefixes and suffixes. Match each word to its correct meaning from Column B.

### COLUMN A

1. ex(pur)gate _____
2. ablution _____
3. lavatory _____
4. deluge _____

5. purge _____
6. purity _____
7. dilution _____

### COLUMN B

a. to cleanse or clear
b. the quality or state of being clean
c. something watered down; less concentrated
d. a washing of the body, especially as a religious ceremony
e. to edit, to censor
f. a room equipped with toilet facilities
g. an overwhelming, flood-like rush

**DIRECTIONS:** Choose the best word from Column A for each sentence. Use each word only once.

1. He was given ample opportunity to _____ himself of all charges.

2. The faucets on the sink in the _____ were of vintage quality.

3. Tanya's grandmother used an old-fashioned _____ of vinegar and water to clean her floors.

4. The school board would need to _____ the film before showing it in the elementary schools.

5. The Pharisees carried the practice of _____ to excess, thus claiming extraordinary _____.

6. The _____ of spam over the Internet can be a nuisance to people.

# FOCUS: magn/magni

| PREFIX | ROOT | | SUFFIX | |
|---|---|---|---|---|
| | **anim** | spirit, life | **-ate** | to make, to act, one who, that which |
| | **loqu** | speak | fic-**ation** | an action or process |
| | **magn/** | great, large | **-ence/** | state, quality, act |
| | **magni** | | fic-**ence** | |
| | | | **-fy** | to act, to do, to make |
| | | | **-ous** | having the quality of |
| | | | **-tude** | state, quality, act |

**DIRECTIONS:** In Column A, identify the parts of each word by circling roots and then underlining prefixes and suffixes. Match each word to its correct meaning from Column B.

**COLUMN A**

1. (magn)ate _____
2. magnification _____
3. magnitude _____
4. magnificence _____
5. magniloquence _____
6. magnify _____
7. magnanimous _____

**COLUMN B**

a. splendid or grand in size or appearance
b. excessive use of verbal ornamentation; pompous discourse
c. to increase in size; enlarge
d. generous, noble, and understanding in spirit
e. a person of high rank, power, influence, etc. in a specific field
f. greatness of size, volume, or extent
g. the process of making something look bigger than it really is

**DIRECTIONS:** Choose the best word from Column A for each sentence. Use each word only once.

1. If you were to _____ your skin, you would see lots of little bumps and holes.

2. Scientists accurately predicted the _____ of the earthquake.

3. Both the losing team and its manager were _____ in their defeat.

4. Gina's father was a famous author and real estate _____.

5. The intricate details of the leaves were seen clearly by _____.

6. The highlight of our trip to Egypt was seeing the grandeur and _____ of the Pyramids.

7. The news anchor was famous for his _____ of style.

# FOCUS: medi

| PREFIX | ROOT | SUFFIX | |
|---|---|---|---|
| inter- between, among | ev age, time<br>medi half, halfway between, middle<br>terr earth | -al | like, related to; an action or process |
| | | -an | like, related to |
| | | -anean | having the quality of |
| | | -ary | that which; someone or something that belongs to; of, related to; one who |
| | | -ate | to make, to act; one who, that which |
| | | -ation | an action or process |

**DIRECTIONS:** In Column A, identify the parts of each word by circling roots and then underlining prefixes and suffixes. Match each word to its correct meaning from Column B.

### COLUMN A

1. (med i)ation _____
2. intermediary _____
3. median _____
4. mediterranean _____
5. intermediate _____
6. medieval _____

### COLUMN B

a. enclosed or nearly enclosed with land
b. relating or belonging to the Middle Ages
c. related to or situated in the middle
d. the process of resolving differences
e. being or happening between two other related things, levels, or points
f. a negotiator who acts as a link between parties

**DIRECTIONS:** Choose the best word from Column A for each sentence. Use each word only once.

1. He acted as an _____ between the police and the sniper.

2. In _____ times, common herbs had great medicinal value.

3. When last minute attempts at _____ failed, the workers went on strike.

4. Jonathan was studying German and Russian at the _____ level.

5. We visited a quaint, _____ village in Spain.

6. Their family's annual income fell in the _____ range.

# FOCUS: melan, mnem/mnes

| PREFIX | | ROOT | | SUFFIX | |
|---|---|---|---|---|---|
| **a-** | away, from; not, without | **chol** | bile, gall | **-ia** | condition |
| | | **crypto** | hidden | **on-ic** | like, related to |
| | | **melan** | black, dark | **-in** | thing which, like, related to |
| | | **mnem/ mnes** | remember, memory | **-oma** | growth, tumor |
| | | | | **t-y** | state of, quality, act; body, group |

**DIRECTIONS:** In Column A, identify the parts of each word by circling roots and then underlining prefixes and suffixes. Match each word to its correct meaning from Column B.

**COLUMN A**

1. (melan)o m a _____
2. a m n e s i a _____
3. m n e m o n i c _____
4. c r y p t o m n e s i a _____
5. a m n e s t y _____
6. m e l a n c h o l y _____
7. m e l a n i n _____

**COLUMN B**

a. characterized by or expressing sadness; gloomy

b. a condition whereby experiences are believed to be original, but are actually based on memories of forgotten events

c. a brownish-black pigment found in skin, hair, and other tissues

d. pardon; literally "forgetting a crime"

e. loss of the ability to remember

f. a type of skin cancer that appears as a dark mark or growth on the skin, eye, and other tissues

g. a short rhyme, phrase, etc. for making information easier to remember

**DIRECTIONS:** Choose the best word from Column A for each sentence. Use each word only once.

1. _____ is sometimes used as an explanation for paranormal events such as xenoglossy or past-life experiences.

2. Freckles and moles form where there is a greater concentration of _____ in the skin.

3. Roberta sang the song in a _____ voice.

4. Experts claim that _____ may be caused by excessive exposure to the sun.

5. The students learned to spell "arithmetic" by using the _____, "a rat in the house may eat the ice cream."

6. Following her automobile accident, Alicia suffered from post-traumatic _____.

7. The president granted general _____ to all political prisoners.

# FOCUS: moll/mollusk

| PREFIX | ROOT | SUFFIX | |
|---|---|---|---|
| **-e**  out, away, from | **moll/**        soft<br>**moll**usk | ific-**ation**<br>usca-**cide**<br>i-**ent**<br>-**escent**<br>i-**fy** | an action or process<br>kill<br>one who, that which; like, related to<br>becoming, having<br>to make, to act, to do |

**DIRECTIONS:** In Column A, identify the parts of each word by circling roots and then underlining prefixes and suffixes.  Match each word to its correct meaning from Column B.

#### COLUMN A

1. mollescent  _____
2. mollusk  _____
3. emollient  _____
4. mollify  _____
5. molluscacide  _____
6. mollification  _____

#### COLUMN B

a. to soothe the temper of; appease; soften
b. appeasement
c. a chemical pesticide used to kill mollusks
d. something that has a softening or soothing effect
e. softening or tending to soften
f. an invertebrate animal having a soft unsegmented body usually enclosed in a shell

**DIRECTIONS:** Choose the best word from Column A for each sentence.  Use each word only once.

1. The store manager was attempting to _____ the angry customer.

2. A _____ was used to keep the snail population under control.

3. The boss realized that _____ of his staff would occur once they received a raise.

4. They added a _____ agent to the rubber compound to give it more pliability.

5. The cuttlefish is a _____, as is the clam and the oyster.

6. The herbal _____ provided much relief to her sunburned skin.

# FOCUS: narc/narco

| PREFIX | | ROOT | | SUFFIX | |
|---|---|---|---|---|---|
| syn- | with, together | leps | take, seize | t-ic | like, related to |
| | | mania | intense craving | -is | thing which |
| | | narc/ | numbness, stupor | -osis | condition |
| | | narco* | | -y | state of, quality, act; body, group |
| | | thes | to place, to put | | |

**DIRECTIONS:** In Column A, identify the parts of each word by circling roots and then underlining prefixes and suffixes. Match each word to its correct meaning from Column B.

### COLUMN A

1. narcosis _____
2. narcomania _____
3. narcotic _____
4. narcolepsy _____
5. narcosynthesis _____

### COLUMN B

a. a drug used to relieve pain and induce sleep
b. a sleep disorder characterized by sudden and uncontrollable episodes of deep sleep
c. a treatment of neurosis, requiring a patient to be under the influence of a hypnotic drug
d. a state of stupor or greatly reduced activity produced by a drug or other element
e. abnormal craving for a drug to deaden pain

**DIRECTIONS:** Choose the best word from Column A for each sentence. Use each word only once.

1. Following surgery, the doctor prescribed a _____ for the patient.

2. It is the sleep therapist's belief that _____ is attributable to an inability to suppress R.E.M. sleep during waking.

3. The deep sea diver experienced nitrogen _____, which left him feeling euphoric and disoriented.

4. _____ was originally used in acute combat distress cases during World War II.

5. George's _____ continued long after his physical discomfort disappeared.

# FOCUS: ortho

| PREFIX | ROOT | | SUFFIX | |
|---|---|---|---|---|
| | **dont** | teeth | **-ic** | like, related to |
| | **dox** | opinion, praise | **t-ics** | science, related to, system |
| | **ortho** | straight, right | | |
| | **graph** | write, written | **-ist** | one who |
| | **ped** | child | **-y** | state of, quality, act; body, group |
| | **scop** | look at, view, examine | | |

**DIRECTIONS:** In Column A, identify the parts of each word by circling roots and then underlining prefixes and suffixes. Match each word to its correct meaning from Column B.

**COLUMN A**

1. orthodontics _____
2. orthopedist _____
3. orthodox _____
4. orthotics _____
5. orthoscopic _____
6. orthography _____

**COLUMN B**

a. spelling in accord with accepted usage

b. the science that deals with the developing and fitting of medical devices

c. related to seeing an image in correct and normal proportion

d. a specialist in correcting deformities of the skeletal system (especially in children)

e. adhering to what is commonly accepted

f. the branch of dentistry concerned with the prevention or correction of irregularities of the teeth

**DIRECTIONS:** Choose the best word from Column A for each sentence. Use each word only once.

1. Chris's mother took him to an _____ to correct his spinal curvature.

2. The author studied _____ before writing a dictionary.

3. Usually _____ can straighten crooked teeth.

4. Pete had _____ surgery to correct his poor vision.

5. _____ enabled the injured soldiers to walk again.

6. The students needed to take an _____ point of view during their research.

# FOCUS: ox/oxy/oxysm

| PREFIX | | ROOT | | SUFFIX | |
|---|---|---|---|---|---|
| **anti-** | against, opposite | **gen** | cause, birth, race, produce | **id-ant** | one who, that which, state, quality |
| **di-** | two | | | | |
| **par-** | beside, variation | **mor** | stupid | **-ation** | an action or process |
| **per-** | through, very | **ox/** | sharp, acid, acute | | |
| | | **oxy/** | | **-ide** | thing belonging to |
| | | **oxy**sm | | **-on** | quality, state |

**DIRECTIONS:** In Column A, identify the parts of each word by circling roots and then underlining prefixes and suffixes. Match each word to its correct meaning from Column B.

### COLUMN A

1. d i o x i d e _____

2. p a r o x y s m _____

3. a n t i o x i d a n t _____

4. p e r o x i d e _____

5. o x y m o r o n _____

6. o x y g e n a t i o n _____

### COLUMN B

a. a combination of contradictory or incongruous words

b. an oxide containing a relatively high proportion of oxygen

c. a sudden and uncontrollable expression of emotion

d. the process of providing oxygen

e. an oxide containing two atoms of oxygen in the molecule

f. substance that counteracts oxidation

**DIRECTIONS:** Choose the best word from Column A for each sentence. Use each word only once.

1. Hydrogen _____ is a commonly used antiseptic.

2. In describing his brother Henry, Casey used the _____, "learned blockhead."

3. The clown's antics produced a _____ of laughter among the children.

4. Commercially produced carbon _____ is used extensively in fire extinguishers.

5. Laughter is cathartic in that it relieves tension and increases tissue _____.

6. Certain compounds derived from vitamin E are used as an _____ to help guard against food spoilage.

# FOCUS: pater/patri

| PREFIX | | ROOT | | SUFFIX | |
| --- | --- | --- | --- | --- | --- |
| ex- | out, away, from | arch | first, chief, rule | n-al | like, related to; an action or process |
| re- | back, again | pater/ | father | -ate | to make, to act, one who, that which |
| | | patri | | -ation | an action or process |
| | | | | -cide | kill |
| | | | | n-ity | state, quality, act |
| | | | | -mony | state, quality, that which |

**DIRECTIONS:** In Column A, identify the parts of each word by circling roots and then underlining prefixes and suffixes. Match each word to its correct meaning from Column B.

### COLUMN A

1. patriarchal _____
2. paternal _____
3. expatriate _____
4. patricide _____
5. paternity _____
6. repatriation _____
7. patrimony _____

### COLUMN B

a. the killing of a father by his own child
b. the fact or state of being a father; fatherhood
c. the act of returning to one's country of origin
d. relating to or characteristic of a culture ruled by men
e. someone who no longer lives in his or her own country
f. an estate inherited from one's father or ancestor
g. related on the father's side

**DIRECTIONS:** Choose the best word from Column A for each sentence. Use each word only once.

1. The courts determined his rights of _____ through his DNA.

2. Lester was an _____ who emigrated to America during World War II.

3. According to, The Book of Assassins, by George Fetherling, Julius Ceasar's assassination may have been _____.

4. Marcella's _____ grandparents are of Italian descent.

5. The _____ of its refugees was crucial to the rebuilding of the nation.

6. The _____ of the royal family was divided equally among the king's three sons.

7. Many feminist writers believe that _____ principles have been the basis upon which most modern societies have been formed.

# FOCUS: pend/pens

| PREFIX | | ROOT | | SUFFIX | |
|---|---|---|---|---|---|
| **ap-** | to, toward, against | **pend/ pens** | hang, weigh | **-age** | state, quality, act |
| **im-** | in, into; not | | | **-ant** | one who, that which; state, quality |
| **sus-** | up | | | **-ing** | related to |
| | | | | **-ion** | an action or process; state, quality, act |
| | | | | **-ive** | tending to or performing |
| | | | | **-ulous** | having the quality of |

**DIRECTIONS:** In Column A, identify the parts of each word by circling roots and then underlining prefixes and suffixes. Match each word to its correct meaning from Column B.

### COLUMN A

1. (pens)ive _____
2. suspension _____
3. pendant _____
4. impending _____
5. append _____
6. pendulous _____
7. appendage _____

### COLUMN B

a. that is about to occur; imminent
b. to attach; to state further
c. an interruption; literally, "to be left hanging"
d. hanging loosely or swinging freely
e. thoughtfully weighing an issue or problem
f. an ornamental, hanging object
g. a projecting body part; a secondary attachment

**DIRECTIONS:** Choose the best word from Column A for each sentence. Use each word only once.

1. At every session, the legislators continued to _____ amendments to the original proposal.

2. The house was closed up tightly in preparation for an _____ blizzard.

3. As she read the letter, the expression on her face indicated a _____ mood.

4. Their grandfather was a corpulent old man with flabby, _____ jowls.

5. Marc's left leg was his only _____ injured in the accident.

6. Her parents gave her a jeweled _____ as a graduation gift.

7. Because she talked back to her teacher, Jen received a 3-day _____ from school.

# FOCUS: petr/petro

| PREFIX | ROOT | | SUFFIX | |
|--------|------|--|--------|--|
| | **glyph** | carve | l-**eum** | that which |
| | **graph** | write, written | li-**ferous** | producing |
| | **petr/** | rock | i-**fy** | to do, to make, to act |
| | **petro** | | -**ic** | like, related to |
| | | | -**logy** | study of, science |

**DIRECTIONS:** In Column A, identify the parts of each word by circling roots and then underlining prefixes and suffixes. Match each word to its correct meaning from Column B.

**COLUMN A**

1. petroleum _____
2. petroglyph _____
3. petrology _____
4. petrographic _____
5. petrify _____
6. petroliferous _____

**COLUMN B**

a. ancient carving or inscription on rock
b. to turn organic matter into stone
c. containing or yielding petroleum
d. the study of the origin, formation, and composition of rocks
e. crude oil that occurs naturally in sedimentary rocks and consists mainly of hydrocarbons
f. related to the systematic description and classification of rocks using microscopic examination

**DIRECTIONS:** Choose the best word from Column A for each sentence. Use each word only once.

1. Just north of Quito, Ecuador, there is a river that can _____ any sort of wood or leaves.

2. Lunar rocks returned by Apollo astronauts were studied with _____ techniques.

3. The strategy of oil and gas exploration is to focus on undeveloped but potentially _____ basins throughout the world.

4. A wide variety of commercially important petrochemicals like gasoline and kerosene are derived from _____.

5. Fields of specialization in _____ correspond to the three major rock types: igneous, sedimentary, and metamorphic.

6. The scientists studied the cultural and religious significance of the _____ they had copied from the cave.

# FOCUS: phag/phago

| PREFIX | ROOT | | SUFFIX | |
|---|---|---|---|---|
| | **anthropo** | man, mankind | **-ous** | having the quality of |
| | **eso** | to bear, to carry | **-us** | thing which |
| | **ichthyo** | fish | **-y** | state of, quality, act; body, group |
| | **phag/ phago** | eat | | |
| | **phyllo** | leaf | | |
| | **sarco** | flesh | | |
| | **tomy** | cut | | |
| | **xero***  | dry | | |

**DIRECTIONS:** In Column A, identify the parts of each word by circling roots and then underlining prefixes and suffixes. Match each word to its correct meaning from Column B.

**COLUMN A**

1. (eso)(phag)(tomy) _____
2. ichthyophagous _____
3. xerophagy _____
4. sarcophagus _____
5. anthropophagous _____
6. esophagus _____
7. phyllophagous _____

**COLUMN B**

a. the part of the digestive tract that connects the throat to the stomach (Medical)
b. feeding on leaves; leaf-eating
c. feeding on human flesh; cannibalistic
d. incision through the wall of the esophagus (Medical)
e. eating of dry food
f. fish-eating
g. an ornamental stone coffin used to decompose the flesh of the corpse within

**DIRECTIONS:** Choose the best word from Column A for each sentence. Use each word only once.

1. The class was fascinated by the story of Christopher Columbus's encounter with the Caribs, a presumedly _____ culture.

2. The _____ stick insects camouflage themselves, making it difficult for predators to spot them.

3. Among the great archaeological finds was an alabaster _____ of an Egyptian pharaoh.

4. The boy's life was saved by an emergency _____ to remove the obstruction.

5. Greenland Eskimos attribute their lower rate of cardiovascular disease to a highly _____ diet.

6. _____ in the week preceding Easter constitutes the strictest fast in the Eastern Orthodox Church.

7. When a person swallows, the muscular walls of the _____ contract to push food down into the stomach.

# FOCUS: phys

| PREFIX | | ROOT | | SUFFIX | |
|---|---|---|---|---|---|
| **meta-** | beyond, change | **phys** | nature, growth | ic-**al** | like, related to; an action or process |
| | | | | ic-**ian** | one who |
| | | | | -**ics** | science, related to, system |
| | | | | ic-**ist** | one who |
| | | | | ical-**ly** | in the manner of |
| | | | | i-**ology** | study of, science |

**DIRECTIONS:** In Column A, identify the parts of each word by circling roots and then underlining prefixes and suffixes. Match each word to its correct meaning from Column B.

**COLUMN A**

1. (phys)iology  _____
2. physicist  _____
3. metaphysics  _____
4. physician  _____
5. physics  _____
6. physically  _____
7. physical  _____

**COLUMN B**

a. a branch of philosophy dealing with the nature of reality
b. in a physical manner; in respect to the body
c. related to matter and energy and their interactions
d. of or relating to the body
e. a scientist whose specialty is physics
f. a person skilled in the art of healing
g. the branch of the biological sciences that deals with the functioning of organisms

**DIRECTIONS:** Choose the best word from Column A for each sentence. Use each word only once.

1. His goal as a _____ is to help people achieve good health.

2. Dennis believes his _____ strength is due to good genes.

3. Modern scientific disciplines include areas such as quantum mechanics, relativity, and nuclear _____.

4. Since the discovery of the cell structure of tissues, _____ has undergone rapid development.

5. _____ often poses questions regarding the existence and nature of the universe.

6. The accomplished _____ lectured on thermodynamics and electromagnetism.

7. The ptarmigan, chinchilla, and snowshoe rabbit are animals that are _____ adapted to living in alpine regions.

# FOCUS: phyte/phyto

| PREFIX | ROOT | | SUFFIX | |
|--------|------|--|--------|--|
| | **chrome** | color | **-ic** | like, related to |
| | **cryo**\* | cold | **-logy** | study of, science |
| | **gen** | cause, birth, produce, race | **-ous** | having the quality of |
| | **morph** | form | **-y** | state of, quality, act; body, group |
| | **patho** | feeling, disease | | |
| | **phag** | eat | | |
| | **phyte/phyto** | plant | | |
| | **therap** | treatment | | |

**DIRECTIONS:** In Column A, identify the parts of each word by circling roots and then underlining prefixes and suffixes. Match each word to its correct meaning from Column B.

### COLUMN A

1. (phyto)(phag)ous _____

2. phytology _____
3. phytochrome _____

4. cryophyte _____
5. phytomorphic _____
6. phytotherapy _____
7. phytopathogen _____

### COLUMN B

a. the pigment in green plants that absorbs light and controls dormancy, flowering, and the germination of seeds
b. having attributes of a plant
c. the use of herbs and other plants to promote health and treat disease
d. something that causes disease in plants
e. a plant that can live or grow on snow or ice
f. the study of plants; botany
g. plant-eating; herbivorous

**DIRECTIONS:** Choose the best word from Column A for each sentence. Use each word only once.

1. Colonies of _____ bryozoans or moss animals arise from the continual budding of the cells.

2. Aromatic vegetable oil extracts have been an integral part of _____ as far back as 2000 B.C.

3. The new strain of bacterial _____ destroyed the entire corn crop.

4. The diverse regions of Big Bend National Park in Texas are an ideal place for _____ classes to study desert plants.

5. The _____ mirid or leaf bug is found on much of the vegetation throughout Canada.

6. Any species of mold that can adapt to low temperatures is a _____.

7. _____ enhances the rate of chlorophyll accumulation in certain seedlings.

# FOCUS: plac

| PREFIX | | ROOT | | SUFFIX | |
|---|---|---|---|---|---|
| **com-** | with, together | **plac** | please, soothe, gentle | **-able** | able to be |
| **im-** | in, into; not | | | **-ate** | to make, to act; one who, that which |
| | | | | **-ebo** | something tending to |
| | | | | **-ent** | like, related to; one who, that which |
| | | | | **-id** | like, related to |
| | | | | **-ity** | state, quality, act |

**DIRECTIONS:** In Column A, identify the parts of each word by circling roots and then underlining prefixes and suffixes. Match each word to its correct meaning from Column B.

### COLUMN A

1. placid _____
2. placate _____
3. implacable _____
4. placebo _____
5. complacent _____
6. placidity _____

### COLUMN B

a. to soothe or mollify; appease
b. the quality or feeling of being calm or composed
c. overly pleased with oneself or one's situation; smug
d. not capable of being appeased or pacified
e. calm in nature; tranquil
f. something done or said simply to reassure

**DIRECTIONS:** Choose the best word from Column A for each sentence. Use each word only once.

1. The soldier realized they were facing an _____ enemy.

2. The journalist had become too _____ after many years of success.

3. After the storm, the lake was so _____ it looked like glass.

4. Pressure was placed on the politician to _____ the voters he represented.

5. Her father's _____ only further antagonized the rebellious teenager.

6. His kind gesture acted as a _____ in her time of need.

# FOCUS: pon/pone

| PREFIX | | ROOT | | SUFFIX | |
|---|---|---|---|---|---|
| **com-** | with, together | **pon/** | place, put | **i-al** | like, related to; an action or process |
| **ex-** | out, away, from | **pone** | | | |
| **op-** | to, toward, against | | | **-ent** | one who, that which; like, related to |
| **post-** | after | | | | |
| **pro-** | for, before, forward | | | **-ment** | that which |

**DIRECTIONS:** In Column A, identify the parts of each word by circling roots and then underlining prefixes and suffixes. Match each word to its correct meaning from Column B.

### COLUMN A

1. post(pon)ement  _____
2. opponent  _____
3. component  _____
4. proponent  _____
5. postpone  _____
6. exponential  _____

### COLUMN B

a. one who argues in favor of something; advocate
b. to put something off until a later time; delay
c. one who takes an opposite position; rival
d. characterized by an extremely rapid increase
e. the act of putting something off to a future time
f. a part of something larger

**DIRECTIONS:** Choose the best word from Column A for each sentence. Use each word only once.

1. Jared supported and was a strong _____ of the bill which would approve national health insurance.

2. We've had to _____ our trip twice due to unexpected illness.

3. The _____ rise in disease was caused by an increase in the mosquito population.

4. Inclement weather was responsible for the _____ of the tennis match.

5. After the game, Jessica's _____ congratulated her on her win.

6. Each separate _____ of the computer had to fit perfectly.

# FOCUS: pter/ptero

| PREFIX | ROOT | | SUFFIX | |
|---|---|---|---|---|
| **a-**    away, from; not, without | **brachy***   short **pter/** **ptero**   wing, feather **saur**   lizard | | **ygi-al** **yg-oid** **id-ology** **-ous** | like, related to; an action or process resembling study of, science having the quality of |

**DIRECTIONS:** In Column A, identify the parts of each word by circling roots and then underlining prefixes and suffixes. Match each word to its correct meaning from Column B.

### COLUMN A

1. (brachy)(pter)ous    _____
2. pterosaur    _____
3. pterygoid    _____
4. apterygial    _____
5. pteridology    _____

### COLUMN B

a. extinct flying reptile
b. belonging to the group of animals without paired wings, fins, or limbs
c. the branch of botany that studies ferns
d. short winged
e. like a bird's wing in form

**DIRECTIONS:** Choose the best word from Column A for each sentence. Use each word only once.

1. _____ beetles cannot fly and rarely disperse long distances.

2. The students of _____ took photographs of a variety of pressed ferns.

3. The _____ cyclostomi are elongated creatures resembling eels.

4. Like the dinosaur, the _____ was affected by the mass extinction at the end of the Cretaceous Period.

5. The _____ muscles in the skull, when inflamed, can interfere with chewing, talking, and range of motion.

# FOCUS:  pyret/pyreto, pyro

| PREFIX | | ROOT | | SUFFIX | |
|---|---|---|---|---|---|
| **a-** | away, from; not, without | **gen** | cause, birth, produce, race | **-ic** | like, related to |
| **anti-** | against, opposite | **pyret/ pyreto***  | fever | **-osis** | condition |
| | | **pyro*** | fire, heat | **-y** | state of, quality, act; body, group |
| | | **therap** | treatment | | |
| | | **typh** | stupor, fog | | |

**DIRECTIONS:** In Column A, identify the parts of each word by circling roots and then underlining prefixes and suffixes.  Match each word to its correct meaning from Column B.

### COLUMN A

1. pyretotherapy _____
2. apyretic _____
3. pyrogenic _____
4. antipyretic _____
5. pyretotyphosis _____

### COLUMN B

a.  drug that relieves or reduces fever
b.  the delirium of fever
c.  fever therapy
d.  fever-inducing
e.  without fever

**DIRECTIONS:** Choose the best word from Column A for each sentence.  Use each word only once.

1. Tylenol™ is a common _____.

2. When Maria's body temperature reached 105 degrees, _____ and subsequent unconsciousness occurred.

3. The  pediatrician said that Billy could return to school as soon as he was _____.

4. _____ causes a fundamental change in the internal environment of the body.

5. Coley's toxin was a _____ vaccine developed to treat and reduce cancerous tumors.

# FOCUS: secute/sequ

| PREFIX | | ROOT | SUFFIX | |
|---|---|---|---|---|
| **con-** | with, together | **secute/** follow | **i-al** | like, related to; an action or process |
| **non-** | not | **sequ** | | |
| **ob-** | to, toward, against | | **-ence** | state, quality, act |
| **per-** | through, very | | **-ent** | one who, that which; like, related to |
| **pro-** | for, before, forward | | **i-ous** | having the quality of |
| **sub-** | under, below | | **it-ur** | that which |

**DIRECTIONS:** In Column A, identify the parts of each word by circling roots and then underlining prefixes and suffixes. Match each word to its correct meaning from Column B.

### COLUMN A

1. con(sequ)ence _____
2. prosecute _____
3. obsequious _____
4. non sequitur _____
5. persecute _____
6. sequential _____
7. subsequent _____

### COLUMN B

a. a remark having no bearing on what has just been said
b. overly eager to please or obey
c. happening or existing after; later
d. to take legal action and bring someone before a court
e. the effect, result, or outcome of something occurring earlier
f. following in regular succession without gaps
g. to oppress; to pester continually

**DIRECTIONS:** Choose the best word from Column A for each sentence. Use each word only once.

1. The legislature convenes on _____ days each week.

2. We had been discussing plumbing, so Elizabeth's remark about astrology was a real _____.

3. The accident was the unfortunate _____ of reckless driving.

4. The store manager stated that she would _____ anyone found shoplifting.

5. She complained that he continued to _____ her even after the police had intervened.

6. His _____ attitude was irritating to those around him.

7. The noise intensified with each _____ explosion.

# FOCUS: sec/sicc

| PREFIX | | ROOT | | SUFFIX | |
| --- | --- | --- | --- | --- | --- |
| **de-** | from, away, down, apart, not | **sec/ sicc** | dry | **-ant** | one who, that which; state, quality |
| **demi-** | half | | | **-ate** | to make, to act; one who, that which |
| | | | | **-ation** | an action or process |
| | | | | at**-ive** | tending to or performing |

**DIRECTIONS:** In Column A, identify the parts of each word by circling roots and then underlining prefixes and suffixes.  Match each word to its correct meaning from Column B.

### COLUMN A

1. de(sicc)ation          _____
2. desiccant           _____
3. siccative           _____
4. desiccate           _____
5. demi-sec            _____

### COLUMN B

a.  to dry completely; to deprive of moisture
b.  half-dry; semi-dry
c.  the process of extracting moisture
d.  a substance that promotes drying
e.  causing to dry; drying

**DIRECTIONS:** Choose the best word from Column A for each sentence.  Use each word only once.

1. Calcium oxide is a _____ agent used in paints to accelerate the drying process.

2. They chose a _____champagne to have with their dinner.

3. The partial _____ of landlocked seas at many stages of geological history has caused deposits of gypsum and rock salt.

4. Agricultural herbicides tend to damage leaf cells and to _____ plants.

5. Silica gel is a _____ commonly used to collect and hold moisture in refrigeration and air conditioning systems.

# FOCUS: selen/seleno

| PREFIX | ROOT | | SUFFIX | |
|---|---|---|---|---|
| | **centr** | center | **-er** | one who, that which |
| | **dont** | tooth | | |
| | **graph** | write, written | **-ic** | like, related to |
| | **scop** | look at, view, examine | **-ium** | chemical element |
| | | | **-logy** | study of, science |
| | **selen/** | moon, brightness | **-osis** | condition |
| | **seleno** | | | |

**DIRECTIONS:** In Column A, identify the parts of each word by circling roots and then underlining prefixes and suffixes. Match each word to its correct meaning from Column B.

### COLUMN A

1. (selen)osis _____
2. selenographer _____
3. selenodont _____
4. selenology _____
5. selenocentric _____
6. selenium _____
7. selenoscope _____

### COLUMN B

a. the study of the origin and physical characteristics of the moon
b. a trace mineral that has light-sensitive properties
c. instrument for viewing the moon
d. of or relating to the center of the moon; having the moon as center
e. having molars with crowns formed of crescent-shaped cusps
f. expert in mapping the physical features of the moon
g. poisoning caused by ingesting dangerously high amounts of selenium

**DIRECTIONS:** Choose the best word from Column A for each sentence. Use each word only once.

1. Many herbivorous mammals possess _____ teeth, which make it easier for them to feed on abrasive substances.

2. When frogs are discolored yellow, that indicates a deficiency of _____.

3. _____ orbits are among the five orbital classes used in the search for extraterrestrial artifacts.

4. Much of the land in the Great Plains region is useless for grazing due to the danger of _____.

5. Robert Hooke, a leading developer of instruments during the 1600's, fabricated a _____ specifically for lunar use.

6. The _____ explained that the moon's atmosphere extends three miles above its surface and that it has sufficient density to support vegetation.

7. The findings of lunar missions and _____ have shown the earth and moon to have remarkably similar characteristics.

# FOCUS: surg/surrect, traumat

| PREFIX | | ROOT | | SUFFIX | |
|---|---|---|---|---|---|
| **in-** | in, into; not | **surg/** | rise | **-ence** | state, quality, act |
| **post-** | after | **surrect** | | **-ent** | one who, that which; like, related to |
| **re-** | back, again | **traumat** | shock or wound | **-ic** | like, related to |
| | | | | **-ion** | an action or process; state, quality, act |
| | | | | **-ize** | to make, to act |

**DIRECTIONS:** In Column A, identify the parts of each word by circling roots and then underlining prefixes and suffixes. Match each word to its correct meaning from Column B.

### COLUMN A

1. in(surg)ent   _____
2. traumatic   _____
3. resurgence   _____
4. traumatize   _____
5. insurrection   _____
6. post-traumatic   _____

### COLUMN B

a. occurring as a result of or after injury
b. a rising up against established authority
c. person involved in a rebellion against a constituted authority
d. relating to a physical or emotional wound
e. to cause somebody to experience severe emotional distress
f. a rising again into life, activity, or prominence

**DIRECTIONS:** Choose the best word from Column A for each sentence. Use each word only once.

1. The commandos planning the _____ swore the participants to secrecy.

2. Years later, the _____ incident still made her frightened of the dark.

3. After the attack, the belligerent _____ was found hiding in hills surrounding the town.

4. There is a huge _____ of phonics being taught in schools throughout America.

5. Following wartime combat, many veterans suffer from _____ stress disorder.

6. Violent behavior in the home environment will assuredly _____ children.

# FOCUS: tachisto/tachy

| PREFIX | ROOT | | SUFFIX | |
|---|---|---|---|---|
| | **card** | heart | **-ia** | condition |
| | **graph** | write, written | **-on** | quality, state |
| | **meter** | measure | **-y** | state of, quality, act; body, group |
| | **phras** | speech | | |
| | **scope** | look at, view, examine | | |
| | **tachisto/** | fast | | |
| | **tachy** | | | |

**DIRECTIONS:** In Column A, identify the parts of each word by circling roots and then underlining prefixes and suffixes. Match each word to its correct meaning from Column B.

**COLUMN A**

1. (tachisto)(scope) _____
2. t a c h y o n _____
3. t a c h y m e t e r _____
4. t a c h y c a r d i a _____
5. t a c h y g r a p h y _____
6. t a c h y p h r a s i a _____

**COLUMN B**

a. an abnormally fast heartbeat
b. the art or technique of rapid writing or shorthand
c. a hypothetical subatomic particle that can travel faster than the speed of light
d. abnormally rapid yet fluent and articulate speech
e. instrument for rapidly showing images on a screen to test perception
f. device for measuring speed of rotation

**DIRECTIONS:** Choose the best word from Column A for each sentence. Use each word only once.

1. The _____ plays a large role in science fiction stories that involve time travel.

2. _____ dates back to medieval times, but the first stenographic system worthy of note appeared in England in 1627.

3. Daniel was promoted to news anchor because his _____ works well on TV.

4. The teacher used a _____ to encourage her students to read faster.

5. The cardiologist performed an ablation to treat Ernie's supraventricular _____.

6. The _____ in the Swiss watch was calibrated in miles per hour.

# FOCUS: ten

|  | PREFIX | ROOT | | SUFFIX | |
|---|---|---|---|---|---|
| **de-** | from, away, down, apart, not | **ten** | hold | **-able** | able to be |
| **re-** | back, again | | | **-acious** | having the quality of |
| **un-** | not | | | t**-ive** | tending to or performing |
| | | | | **-tion** | state, quality, act |
| | | | | **-ure** | state, quality, act; that which; process, condition |

**DIRECTIONS:** In Column A, identify the parts of each word by circling roots and then underlining prefixes and suffixes. Match each word to its correct meaning from Column B.

### COLUMN A

1. (ten)able _____
2. detention _____
3. tenure _____
4. tenacious _____
5. retentive _____
6. untenable _____

### COLUMN B

a. the term during which some position is held
b. tending to retain or hold on to
c. not able to be defended or justified
d. able to be held for a specified time
e. the act of detaining or holding back
f. holding firmly to one's position, opinion, etc.

**DIRECTIONS:** Choose the best word from Column A for each sentence. Use each word only once.

1. Bernie claims his success in school was due to a _____ memory.

2. During his _____ as principal, the high school excelled in all academic areas.

3. Recent discoveries made his theory _____.

4. Selena was granted a university fellowship _____ for three years.

5. Julie's homeroom teacher was in charge of the _____ of tardy pupils.

6. The residents have been _____ in their opposition to the new airport.

# FOCUS: tme/tom/tome/tomy

| PREFIX | | ROOT | | SUFFIX | |
|---|---|---|---|---|---|
| **a-** | away, from, not, without | **appendec** | supplement, appendage | **-ize** | to make, to act |
| **ana-** | back, against | **micro*** | small | **-sis** | action, process |
| **epi-** | on, outside | **tme/ tom/ tome/ tomy** | cut | | |

**DIRECTIONS:** In Column A, identify the parts of each word by circling roots and then underlining prefixes and suffixes. Match each word to its correct meaning from Column B.

**COLUMN A**

1. epi(tome)  _____
2. anatomy  _____
3. appendectomy  _____
4. tmesis  _____
5. atomize  _____
6. microtome  _____

**COLUMN B**

a. separation of a compound word by interposition of another word
b. to reduce to minute particles
c. a summary or typical example of something
d. scientific instrument that cuts thin slices of biological tissues for microscopic examination
e. the scientific study of the body and how its parts are arranged
f. the surgical removal of the appendix

**DIRECTIONS:** Choose the best word from Column A for each sentence. Use each word only once.

1. Della had an emergency _____ last year which saved her life.

2. TNT was used to _____ the bridge.

3. The _____ provided a biopsy sample that was a few millionths of a meter thick.

4. An accurate drawing of the human body requires some knowledge of _____.

5. Even in her mid-sixties, Ramona is the _____ of elegance and class.

6. In the English language, it is extremely rare to find a _____, such as "be thou ware."

# FOCUS: trude/trus

| PREFIX | | ROOT | | SUFFIX | |
|---|---|---|---|---|---|
| **ex-** | out, away, from | **trude/** | thrust | **-ion** | an action or process; state, quality, act |
| **in-** | in, into; not | **trus** | | | |
| **ob-** | to, toward, against | | | **-ive** | tending to or performing |
| **pro-** | for, before, forward | | | | |
| **un-** | not | | | | |

**DIRECTIONS:** In Column A, identify the parts of each word by circling roots and then underlining prefixes and suffixes. Match each word to its correct meaning from Column B.

### COLUMN A

1. pro(trus)ive    _____
2. intrude    _____
3. protrude    _____
4. extrusion    _____
5. unobtrusive    _____
6. intrusion    _____

### COLUMN B

a. inconspicuous; not standing out
b. jutting or thrusting forward
c. the action of squeezing something out by pressure
d. to bulge or extend forward
e. to enter uninvited
f. a disturbance; an invasion of someone's privacy

**DIRECTIONS:** Choose the best word from Column A for each sentence. Use each word only once.

1. The _____ of glue from the tube covered a small part of the surface.

2. In the distance we can see several rocks that _____ from the cliff.

3. It was rude of them to _____ on the private dinner party.

4. He entered the classroom trying to be as _____ as possible.

5. Beth mistakenly felt that her presence in their home was an _____.

6. Only in slow motion could we see the frog's _____ tongue snatch the insect.

# FOCUS: verm/vermi

| PREFIX | ROOT | | SUFFIX | |
|---|---|---|---|---|
| | **fug** | flee | **-al** | like, related to; an action or process |
| | **phob** | fear of | **-celli** | small |
| | **verm/** | worm | **-cide** | kill |
| | **vermi** | | **-ia** | condition |
| | **vor** | eat | **-in** | thing which; like, related to |
| | | | **-ous** | having the quality of |

**DIRECTIONS:** In Column A, identify the parts of each word by circling roots and then underlining prefixes and suffixes. Match each word to its correct meaning from Column B.

| COLUMN A | | COLUMN B |
|---|---|---|
| 1. vermivorous | _____ | a. fear of worms |
| 2. vermicide | _____ | b. any of various small animals or insects that are pests; e.g., cockroaches or rats |
| 3. vermiphobia | _____ | c. pasta in strings thinner than spaghetti |
| 4. vermin | _____ | d. tending to expel worms |
| 5. vermicelli | _____ | e. a substance used to kill worms |
| 6. verminous | _____ | f. of the nature of vermin; very offensive or repulsive |
| 7. vermifugal | _____ | g. feeding on worms |

**DIRECTIONS:** Choose the best word from Column A for each sentence. Use each word only once.

1. The chef prepared a dish consisting of _____ with basil and sun-dried tomatoes.

2. The abandoned building was infested with all kinds of _____, especially rats.

3. The _____ garbage collecting in the dump station is a health hazard to the community.

4. Some people have _____, but spiders are what I fear most.

5. The flood plains of the Netherlands are an important foraging area for several species of _____ animals.

6. The veterinarian treated our dog for intestinal parasites with a _____ medication.

7. Naphthalene is a commonly used commercial _____.

# FOCUS: visc/visco

| PREFIX | ROOT | | SUFFIX | |
|---|---|---|---|---|
| | **elast** | expansive | **ic-ity** | state, quality, act |
| | **meter** | measure | **s-ity** | state, quality, act |
| | **visc/** | sticky | **id-ly** | in the manner of |
| | **visco** | | **-ous** | having the quality of |

**DIRECTIONS:** In Column A, identify the parts of each word by circling roots and then underlining prefixes and suffixes. Match each word to its correct meaning from Column B.

## COLUMN A

1. (visc)ous          _____
2. viscosity          _____
3. viscometer          _____
4. viscidly          _____
5. viscoelasticity          _____

## COLUMN B

a. instrument for measuring viscosity
b. in a sticky manner
c. thick and sticky; not free-flowing
d. being both viscous and elastic simultaneously
e. thickness of a liquid or its resistance to flow

**DIRECTIONS:** Choose the best word from Column A for each sentence. Use each word only once.

1. Larry could feel the blood move _____ from his badly cut scalp as it trickled down his forehead.

2. The _____ of certain asphalt makes it ideal for use in road surfacing, roofing, and waterproofing.

3. Diesel fuels are more _____ than gasoline.

4. The plastics industry helps assure the consistency, safety, and durability of their products by using a _____.

5. Cold honey has a much higher _____ than water.

# FOCUS: xer/xero

| PREFIX | ROOT | | SUFFIX | |
|---|---|---|---|---|
| | **derma** | skin | **-ia** | condition |
| | **graph** | write, written | **-ic** | like, related to |
| | **ophthalm** | eye | **-y** | state of, quality, act; body, group |
| | **phyte** | plant | | |
| | **therm** | heat | | |
| | **xer/** | dry | | |
| | **xero\*** | | | |

**DIRECTIONS:** In Column A, identify the parts of each word by circling roots and then underlining prefixes and suffixes. Match each word to its correct meaning from Column B.

| COLUMN A | | COLUMN B |
|---|---|---|
| 1. xerography _____ | | a. abnormal dryness of the skin (Medical) |
| 2. xerothermic _____ | | b. related to electrophotography or dry photocopying |
| 3. xerophyte _____ | | c. excessive dryness of the conjunctiva and cornea of the eye (Medical) |
| 4. xeroderma _____ | | d. method of dry photocopying in which the image is transferred by using the forces of electric charges |
| 5. xerophthalmia _____ | | e. of or pertaining to a hot and dry climactic period |
| 6. xerographic _____ | | f. a plant structurally adapted for growth in dry conditions |

**DIRECTIONS:** Choose the best word from Column A for each sentence. Use each word only once.

1. Proper treatment for Kayla's _____ consisted of mega-doses of vitamin A.

2. In 1960, the Haloid-Xerox Company introduced the first push-button, plain-paper _____ office machine.

3. About 8,300 years ago, a _____ era occurred in the grassland region of central North America.

4. Fran's _____ caused much itching, scaling, and freckling.

5. Variations of _____ are used in such devices as laser printers and plain-paper fax machines.

6. The agave is a _____ that thrives well in extreme desert conditions.

# FOCUS: xyl/xylo

| PREFIX | ROOT | | SUFFIX | |
|---|---|---|---|---|
| | **graph** | write, written | **-er** | one who, that which |
| | **phag** | eat | **-logy** | study of, science |
| | **phone** | sound | **-oid** | resembling |
| | **xyl/** | wood | **-ose** | have the quality of, a carbohydrate |
| | **xylo\*** | | **-ous** | having the quality of |

**DIRECTIONS:** In Column A, identify the parts of each word by circling roots and then underlining prefixes and suffixes. Match each word to its correct meaning from Column B.

### COLUMN A

1. xylose _____
2. xylology _____
3. xylographer _____

4. xyloid _____
5. xylophagous _____
6. xylophone _____

### COLUMN B

a. resembling or like wood in nature
b. a sugar extracted from wood
c. a musical instrument of flat, wooden bars of different lengths that produce notes when hit with sticks
d. feeding on wood
e. the study of the structure of wood
f. one who is skilled in artistic wood carving

**DIRECTIONS:** Choose the best word from Column A for each sentence. Use each word only once.

1. Twigs and _____ plants were used for toothbrushes many years ago.

2. Since around 1920, the _____ has been equipped with tubular resonators, essentially making it identical to the marimba.

3. In _____, students learn to identify different woods and to distinguish real wood from imitations.

4. One way to minimize a wood shortage is to protect trees from harmful _____ insects.

5. Natural sweeteners like stevia and _____ are ideal for diabetics because they do not raise blood sugar.

6. The Chinese _____ exhibited printings of Buddhist scripture that he had made from woodcuts.

# Extension Worksheet One

**DIRECTIONS:** Write the letter of the correct definition for each word in Column B.

| COLUMN A | | COLUMN B |
|---|---|---|
| 1. abranchiate | ____ | a. concise |
| 2. anemometer | ____ | b. having a broad flat nose |
| 3. coarctate | ____ | c. measures tactile sensitivity |
| 4. descant | ____ | d. description of flowers |
| 5. antagonistic | ____ | e. measures the acuteness of hearing |
| 6. succinct | ____ | f. pressed together |
| 7. platyrrhine | ____ | g. high melody above the main melody |
| 8. anthography | ____ | h. lacking gills |
| 9. esthesiometer | ____ | i. adversarial |
| 10. acoumeter | ____ | j. wind gauge |

This activity is a review of pages 1–15.

# Extension Worksheet Two

**DIRECTIONS:** Underline the best word to complete each sentence.

1.  The single-owner company underwent a (metamorphosis, hierarchy, paradox) and became a giant franchise.

2.  In black magic, they used a/an (cantillation, incantation, cinematization) to summon the power of darkness.

3.  The (helianthus, anther, anthophyte) is the only root plant native to North America that has gained economic importance.

4.  The newly developed (anesthetic, cephalic, acoustic) device has improved the quality of hearing aids.

5.  Her behavior was the (synthesis, antithesis, kinesthesis) of cowardly.

6.  The surgeon used a general (antithesis, anesthetic, coarctation) on her patient.

7.  The (disturbance, turbidity, combustion) that occurred in the garage was caused by the careless disposal of oily rags.

8.  Calvin's (agoraphobia, concussion, fortitude) caused him to become a recluse.

9.  Methods of (aortarctia, anesthesia, morphology) include drugs, acupuncture, and hypnosis.

10. (Cephalic, Platyhelminth, Platyrrhine) monkeys are known to display considerable paternal care of their young.

This activity is a review of pages 1–15.

# Extension Worksheet Three

**DIRECTIONS:** Circle the word that is spelled correctly in each group of words.

| | | | |
|---|---|---|---|
| 1. | platipus | platypus | platapus |
| 2. | cinerary | cenirary | cinerory |
| 3. | anesthakinesia | anesthekenasia | anesthekinesia |
| 4. | animotropism | anemotropism | anemotrophism |
| 5. | cephalathorax | cephalothoracs | cephalothorax |
| 6. | hieroglyphics | heiroglyphics | heroglyphics |
| 7. | crysanthemum | chrysanthemum | crysanthamum |
| 8. | terbidity | turbidity | tirbidity |
| 9. | isabaric | isobarec | isobaric |
| 10. | orthodox | orthadox | orthodocs |

This activity is a review of pages 1–15.

# Extension Worksheet Four

**DIRECTIONS:** Choose the correct word for each of the following definitions.

1. shapeless:
   a. abranchiate        b. dimorphic        c. amorphous

2. the study of human musculoskeletal movement:
   a. kinesiology        b. morphology        c. anemology

3. to clear from alleged fault or guilt:
   a. inculpate        b. exculpate        c. perturb

4. a narrowing or constriction:
   a. coarctation        b. concussion        c. encephalitis

5. something held as an established opinion:
   a. paradox        b. thesis        c. dogma

6. the action of unaccompanied chanting in free rhythm:
   a. incantation        b. cantillation        c. anesthekinesia

7. harshness or severity of manner or tone:
   a. repercussions        b. asperity        c. turbulence

8. government by clergymen:
   a. hierocracy        b. hieroglyphics        c. hierarchy

9. the principal character in a literary work:
   a. cantatrice        b. aesthete        c. protagonist

10. a flowering plant:
    a. anthophyte        b. chrysanthemum        c. helianthus

This activity is a review of pages 1–15.

# Extension Worksheet Five

**DIRECTIONS:** Write in the letter of the correct definition for each word in Column B.

**COLUMN A**

1. glossolalia ____
2. foliose ____
3. ecstasy ____
4. gregarious ____
5. eolith ____
6. dyspepsia ____
7. cryophilic ____
8. dactylogram ____
9. somniferous ____
10. asphyxiation ____

**COLUMN B**

a. suffocation

b. capable of living at low temperatures

c. fingerprint

d. sleep inducing

e. indigestion

f. overwhelming emotion

g. covered with leaves

h. very early and crude stone tool

i. repetitive non-meaningful speech

j. sociable

This activity is a review of pages 16–30.

# Extension Worksheet Six

**DIRECTIONS:** Underline the best word to complete each sentence.

1. (Eupepsia, Echolalia, Narcohypnia) occurs in normal language development up until 30 months of age.

2. (Cryotherapy, Cryogenics, Dactyloscopy) poses little risk and is ideal for patients who cannot tolerate conventional surgery.

3. Several of the techniques used in (ergonomics, glaciology, metallurgy) are casting, tempering, soldering, and welding.

4. Sufferers of (ergophobia, hypnophobia, glossolalia) typically experience undue and irrational anxiety with respect to the workplace environment.

5. The investigation proved that the victim died by means of (euphoria, asphyxiation, cryoscopy).

6. Jessica received a (felicitation, colloid, dactylogram) from her fellow classmate for being the only one to make the honor roll.

7. (Narcohypnia, Dactylology, Hypnosis) has proven to be quite successful in curing certain addictions.

8. That historical era was politically and culturally (tumultuous, contumacious, gregarious).

9. Joey's decorative (eolith, collage, foliage) won first place.

10. Rita was in charge of public relations based on her (gregarious, echoic, anechoic) nature.

This activity is a review of pages 16–30.

# Extension Worksheet Seven

**DIRECTIONS:** Circle the word that is spelled correctly in each group of words.

| | | | |
|---|---|---|---|
| 1. | holeistic | holistic | holistec |
| 2. | glaciarium | glaciareum | glasiarium |
| 3. | pyrometallergy | pyrometallurgy | pyrametallurgy |
| 4. | sphygmomonamater | sphygmamanometer | sphygmomanometer |
| 5. | crystallize | crystalize | crystalise |
| 6. | ucalyptus | eucaliptus | eucalyptus |
| 7. | tumessence | tumescence | tumescents |
| 8. | pterodactyl | ptyrodactyl | pterodactil |
| 9. | urgonomics | erganomics | ergonomics |
| 10. | Eoanthrapus | Eoanthropus | Eoanthropos |

This activity is a review of pages 16–30.

# Extension Worksheet Eight

**DIRECTIONS:** Choose the correct word for each of the following definitions.

1. the science of communicating by using hand signs:
   a. dactyloscopy      b. dactylology      c. lithography

2. act of congratulating:
   a. felicitation      b. fluctuation      c. ecstasy

3. inflammation of the tongue:
   a. glossolalia      b. epiglottis      c. glossitis

4. having the toes arranged two in front and two behind:
   a. Eocene      b. zygodactyl      c. trophic

5. excessive growth or enlargement of a body part or organ:
   a. atrophy      b. affluence      c. hypertrophy

6. sleepwalker:
   a. somnambulist      b. hypnotist      c. insomniac

7. a means of locating an object using an emitted sound and the reflection back from it:
   a. echolocation      b. echolalia      c. ergonomics

8. the gradual melting away of a glacier from the surface of a landmass:
   a. cryogenics      b. fluctuation      c. deglaciation

9. formed in imitation of some natural sound:
   a. anechoic      b. echoic      c. ergogenic

10. an abundance of material wealth:
    a. fluency      b. affluence      c. tumescence

This activity is a review of pages 16–30.

# Extension Worksheet Nine

**DIRECTIONS:** Write in the letter of the correct definition for each word in Column B..

| COLUMN A | | COLUMN B |
|---|---|---|
| 1. expurgate | ____ | a. imminent |
| 2. melancholy | ____ | b. appease |
| 3. impending | ____ | c. pompous discourse |
| 4. phyllophagous | ____ | d. a fossil fish or fragment of a fish |
| 5. mediterranean | ____ | e. pardon |
| 6. mollify | ____ | f. spelling in accord with accepted usage |
| 7. ichthyolite | ____ | g. enclosed or nearly enclosed with land |
| 8. amnesty | ____ | h. to censor |
| 9. orthography | ____ | i. leaf-eating |
| 10. magniloquence | ____ | j. gloomy |

This activity is a review of pages 31–45.

# Extension Worksheet Ten

**DIRECTIONS:**  Underline the best word to complete each sentence.

1.  The citizens complained that the laws had been changed for the (mediation, mollification, repatriation) of critics.

2.  The widespread use of products made from (petroleum, peroxide, melanin) has created serious environmental problems.

3.  Most cases of (narcolepsy, cryptomnesia, ichthyosis) are treated with topical ointments.

4.  (Petrology, Phytology, Ichthyology) is used in locating the source of the clay from which the ceramic pots were made.

5.  (Anthropophagous, Phyllophagous, Ichthyophagous) insects either remove a part of the leaf or imbibe the fluids on the sap.

6.  Maria's (melanoma, narcomania, narcolepsy) caused her car accident.

7.  New Orleans is famous for the (magniloquence, orthography, magnificence) of its old oak trees.

8.  A/An (oxymoron, mnemonic, paroxysm), such as *cruel kindness*, is often used for dramatic effect.

9.  Albinism is a condition which occurs when a human or an animal is incapable of producing (phytochrome, melanin, ichthyofauna).

10. Vitamins C, E, and the mineral selenium have been proven to have positive (narcotic, magnanimous, antioxidant) effects on humans.

This activity is a review of pages 31–45.

# Extension Worksheet Eleven

**DIRECTIONS:** Circle the word that is spelled correctly in each group of words.

| | | | |
|---|---|---|---|
| 1. | emolient | emolliant | emollient |
| 2. | medieval | medeval | medievel |
| 3. | sarcophagous | sarcophagus | sarcaphagus |
| 4. | ichthyafauna | ichthyofawna | ichthyofauna |
| 5. | mnemonic | nmemonic | mnenonic |
| 6. | orthadontics | orthodontics | orthidontics |
| 7. | narcosynthesize | narcosynthesis | narcosynthises |
| 8. | patriarcal | patriarchil | patriarchal |
| 9. | esophagotomy | esaphagotomy | esophagatomy |
| 10. | cryaphyte | cryophyt | cryophyte |

This activity is a review of pages 31–45.

# Extension Worksheet Twelve

**DIRECTIONS:** Choose the correct word for each of the following definitions.

1. something that has a softening or soothing effect:
   a. narcotic          b. emollient          c. phytopathogen

2. a plant that can live or grow on snow or ice:
   a. cryophyte          b. mollusk          c. ichthyolite

3. a person of high rank, power, influence, etc. in a specific field:
   a. intermediary          b. magnate          c. orthopedist

4. related to matter and energy and their interactions:
   a. orthotics          b. orthodontics          c. physics

5. the act of returning to one's country of origin:
   a. mediation          b. ablution          c. repatriation

6. the fish of a particular region:
   a. ichthyofauna          b. ichthyosaur          c. ichthyolite

7. having attributes of a plant:
   a. phytophagous          b. phytomorphic          c. phyllophagous

8. a type of skin cancer that appears as a dark mark or growth on the skin:
   a. melanin          b. ichthyosis          c. melanoma

9. an oxide containing a relatively high proportion of oxygen:
   a. dioxide          b. peroxide          c. paroxysm

10. botany:
    a. phytology          b. petrology          c. phytotherapy

This activity is a review of pages 31–45.

# Extension Worksheet Thirteen

**DIRECTIONS:** Write in the letter of the correct definition for each word in Column B.

### COLUMN A

1. untenable _____

2. protrusive _____

3. viscidly _____

4. pteridology _____

5. epitome _____

6. siccative _____

7. xerothermic _____

8. placate _____

9. verminous _____

10. proponent _____

### COLUMN B

a. drying

b. summary or typical example of something

c. appease

d. very offensive or repulsive

e. in a sticky manner

f. advocate

g. not able to be defended or justified

h. jutting or thrusting forward

i. the branch of botany that studies ferns

j. of or pertaining to a hot and dry climactic period

This activity is a review of pages 46–61

# Extension Worksheet Fourteen

**DIRECTIONS:** Underline the best word to complete each sentence.

1. Ancient Greek physicians used (selenology, tachygraphy, pyretotherapy) to treat a variety of diseases.

2. The (viscosity, placidity, tenure) of the oil is indicated on every container of motor oil.

3. Thick, fleshy stems or leaves and waxy leaf coatings are characteristic of a (tachyon, xerophyte, pterosaur).

4. The salesman's (obsequious, unobtrusive, placid) behavior often turned potential buyers away.

5. The apartment complex was infested with (vermifugal, xerographic, xylophagous) termites.

6. Pedro's argument for separation of church and state was (tenacious, siccative, sequential) at best.

7. The auto accident was to (placate, traumatize, persecute) Rachael and affect her memory for several years.

8. By the time the ambulance arrived, the elderly man's (tachycardia, tachyphrasia, vermiphobia) had lessened.

9. Asphalt has a consistency varying from (demi-sec, protrusive, viscous) liquid to glossy solid.

10. The two students made their late entrance to class, trying to be as (unobtrusive, untenable, obsequious) as possible.

This activity is a review of pages 46–61.

# Extension Worksheet Fifteen

**DIRECTIONS:** Circle the word that is spelled correctly in each group of words.

1.  apendectomy          appendectomy          appendectome

2.  brachypterous          brochypterous          brachypterus

3.  non sequitor          non sequiter          non sequitur

4.  selenadont          selenodant          selenodont

5.  pyretotyphosis          pyritotyphosis          pyretatyphosis

6.  vermiceli          vermicelli          vermacelli

7.  xylose          xyllose          xyloze

8.  xeropthalmia          xeraphthalmia          xerophthalmia

9.  dessicant          desiccant          desiccent

10.  apterygial          apteryjial          apterigial

This activity is a review of pages 46–61.

# Extension Worksheet Sixteen

**DIRECTIONS:** Choose the correct word for each of the following definitions.

1. the study of the structure of wood:
   a. pteridology            b. xerography            c. xylology

2. drug that relieves or reduces fever:
   a. antipyretic            b. placebo            c. microtome

3. a remark having no bearing on what has just been said:
   a. tachyon            b. tmesis            c. non sequitur

4. like a bird's wing in form:
   a. xyloid            b. pterygoid            c. brachypterous

5. the process of extracting moisture:
   a. insurrection            b. desiccation            c. extrusion

6. abnormal dryness of the skin:
   a. xeroderma            b. selenosis            c. viscoelasticity

7. not capable of being appeased or pacified:
   a. unobtrusive            b. complacent            c. implacable

8. instrument for rapidly showing images on a screen to test perception:
   a. tachistoscope            b. selenoscope            c. tachymeter

9. to reduce to minute particles:
   a. desiccate            b. atomize            c. traumatize

10. the delirium of fever:
    a. selenosis            b. tachyphrasia            c. pyretotyphosis

This activity is a review of pages 46–61.

# Extension Worksheet Seventeen

**DIRECTIONS:** Write a sentence for each of the following words.

1. paradox _____

   _____

2. cephalothorax _____

   _____

3. archetype _____

   _____

4. agoraphobia _____

   _____

5. pterodactyl _____

   _____

6. ergonomics _____

   _____

7. isobaric _____

   _____

8. viscoelasticity _____

   _____

9. Paleolithic _____

   _____

10. anesthekinesia _____

   _____

This activity is a review of pages 1–61.

# Latin Roots for Independent Study

**DIRECTIONS:** Now that you have completed the *Word Roots* activities, see how adept you have become at forming various words from any given root. Add to each word family by forming as many additional words as you can from each of these roots.

(**root** — meaning: *sample word*)

1. **anim** — spirit: *animation* _____

    _____

2. **bib** — to drink: *imbibe* _____

    _____

3. **lev** — lift; raise: *elevator* _____

    _____

4. **mater/matr** — mother: *maternal* _____

    _____

5. **mell**— honey: *mellifluous* _____

    _____

6. **nutr** — to nourish: *malnutrition* _____

    _____

7. **quer** — to complain: *querulous* _____

    _____

8. **sanguin** — blood: *consanguinity* _____

    _____

9. **ubiqu** — everywhere: *ubiquity* _____

    _____

10. **umbr**— shade: *umbrella* _____

    _____

# Greek Roots for Independent Study

**DIRECTIONS:** Now that you have completed the *Word Roots* activities, see how adept you have become at forming various words from any given root. Add to each word family by forming as many additional words as you can from each of these roots.

(**root** — meaning: *sample word*)

1. **bath** — deep: *bathythermograph* _____

   _____

2. **byss** — bottom; depth: *abyss* _____

   _____

3. **chlor** — green: *chlorophyll* _____

   _____

4. **deka** — ten: *triskaidekaphobia* _____

   _____

5. **rhea** — flow; gush: *logorrhea* _____

   _____

6. **erythr** — red: *erythrocyte*_____

   _____

7. **iatr** — healing: *psychiatrist* _____

   _____

8. **ornith** — bird: *ornithology*_____

   _____

9. **etym** — true: *etymology* _____

   _____

10. **zeug/zyg** — yoke; pair: *heterozygous* _____

   _____

# Anglo-Saxon (Old English) Roots for Independent Study

**DIRECTIONS:** Now that you have completed the *Word Roots* activities, see how adept you have become at forming various words from any given root. Add to each word family by forming as many additional words as you can from each of these roots.

(**root** — meaning: *sample word*)

1.  **brew** — to ferment: *brewery* _____
    _____

2.  **fet/fot** — foot: *fetter* _____
    _____

3.  **lern** — to teach: *learning* _____
    _____

4.  **los** — to lose: *loser* _____
    _____

5.  **mark** — boundary; sign: *demarcation* _____
    _____

6.  **rev/rob** — to rob; booty: *robbery* _____
    _____

7.  **shuf** — to push: *shuffle* _____
    _____

8.  **spin** — to spin: *spindle* _____
    _____

9.  **ward** — to protect: *warden* _____
    _____

10. **writh** — to twist: *writhe* _____
    _____

# ANSWER KEY

**Pretest/Posttest, p. vi**

1. **magnanimous**: generous, noble, and understanding in spirit

2. **anemotropism**: orientation in response to air currents

3. **obsequious**: overly eager to please or obey

4. **ichthyofauna**: the fish of a particular region

5. **selenosis**: poisoning caused by ingesting dangerously high amounts of selenium

6. **eucalyptus**: Australian evergreen tree with rigid leaves and protected flowers and having medicinal and industrial value

7. **tmesis**: separation of a compound word by interposition of another word

8. **tumultuous**: full of commotion and uproar

9. **anechoic**: free from echoes and reverberations

10. **ergonomics**: the scientific design of products, machines, etc. to maximize user safety, comfort, and efficiency

11. **exculpate**: to clear from alleged fault or guilt; to free from blame

12. **hypertrophy**: excessisve growth or enlargement of a body part or organ

13. **glossolalia**: repetitive non-meaningful speech

14. **oxymoron**: a combination of contradictory or incongruous words

15. **amorphous**: without definite form; shapeless

16. **vermicelli**: pasta in strings thinner than spaghetti

17. **eolith**: a very early and crude stone tool

18. **implacable**: not capable of being appeased or pacified

19. **mnemonic**: a short rhyme, phrase, etc. for making information easier to remember

20. **pendulous**: hanging loosely or swinging freely

**Warm-up Activity, p. vii**

1. **incombustible**: not capable of being burned

2. **mediation**: the process of resolving differences

3. **somnambulist**: sleepwalker

4. **holocaust**: total or mass destruction

5. **perturb**: to disturb greatly; to upset

6. **appendage**: a projecting body part; a secondary attachment

7. **narcosynthesis**: a treatment of neurosis requiring a patient to be under the influence of a hypnotic drug

**Page 1**

1. e   paradox

2. c   acoustic

3. f   dogma

4. b   acoumeter

5. d   doxology

6. a   orthodox

1. orthodox

2. paradox

3. doxology

4. acoustic

5. acoumeter

6. dogma

**Page 2**

1. e   anesthesia

2. d   anesthetic

3. a   esthesiometer

4. f   aesthete

5. b   anesthesiologist

6. c   aesthetic

1. aesthete

2. aesthetic

3. anesthesia

4. anesthesiologist

5. anesthetic

6. esthesiometer

**Page 3**

1. f   exculpate

2. e   agony

3. d   culpable

4. a   protagonist

5. b   antagonistic

6. c   inculpate

1. inculpate

2. antagonistic

3. agony

4. exculpate

5. protagonist

6. culpable

**Page 4**

1. d fortitude

2. e agora

3. f fortification

4. b comfortable

5. a agoraphobia

6. c fortify

1. agoraphobia

2. fortify

3. fortitude

4. fortification

5. agora

6. comfortable

**Page 5**

1. d barometric

2. g anemometer

3. f isobaric

4. a anemophilous

5. b anemotropism

6. e barometer

7. c anemology

1. anemology

2. anemophilous

3. barometric

4. anemometer

5. isobaric

6. anemotropism

7. barometer

**Page 6**

1. c anthography

2. d anther

3. f helianthus

4. a anthophyte

5. b chrysanthemum

6. e anthophagous

1. anthophyte

2. anthophagous

3. anther

4. chrysanthemum

5. anthography

6. helianthus

**Page 7**

1. e archaic

2. d hierocracy

3. f hierarch

4. b archetype

5. a hieroglyphics

6. c hierarchy

1. archetype

2. hierarchy

3. hieroglyphics

4. hierarch

5. archaic

6. hierocracy

**Page 8**

1. e synthesize

2. c coarctate

3. d antithesis

4. f thesis

5. g aortarctia

6. b antithetic

7. a coarctation

1. thesis

2. antithetic

3. synthesize

4. coarctate

5. antithesis

6. coarctation

7. aortarctia

**Page 9**

1. f exasperation

2. d turbulence

3. e asperity

4. b disturbance

5. a perturb

6. g turbidity

7. c turbine

1. turbulence

2. disturbance

3. perturb

4. turbine

5. exasperation

6. asperity

7. turbidity

**Page 10**

1. d branchial

2. c platypus

3. b abranchiate

4. e platyrrhine

5. a platyhelminth

6. f branchiopod

1. platyhelminth

2. platypus

3. platyrrhine

4. branchial

5. branchiopod

6. abranchiate

**Page 11**

1. b incantation

2. d recant

3. a cantillation

4. e canticle

5. f cantatrice

6. c descant

1. canticle

2. descant

3. incantation

4. recant

5. cantillation

6. cantatrice

## Page 12

1. f    dimorphic

2. e    cephalic

3. b    morphology

4. a    metamorphosis

5. d    amorphous

6. g    encephalitis

7. c    cephalothorax

1. morphology

2. amorphous

3. dimorphic

4. encephalitis

5. cephalic

6. cephalothorax

7. metamorphosis

## Page 13

1. f    succinct

2. e    percussion

3. b    cincture

4. a    concussion

5. c    precinct

6. d    repercussions

1. concussion

2. precinct

3. succinct

4. percussion

5. repercussions

6. cincture

## Page 14

1. f    kinetic

2. g    anesthekinesia

3. a    kinesthesis

4. b    cinematography

5. c    kinesiology

6. d    cinematization

7. e    cinematic

1. cinematization

2. kinesiology

3. cinematic

4. kinetic

5. anesthekinesia

6. cinematography

7. kinesthesis

## Page 15

1. d    incombustible

2. e    incinerator

3. a    combustion

4. b    cinerary

5. c    combustible

1. incinerator

2. cinerary

3. incombustible

4. combustible

5. combustion

## Page 16

1. e    asphyxiation

2. d    collage

3. f    sphygmic

4. a    colloid

5. b    sphygmomanometer

6. c    collagenous

1. sphygmomanometer

2. colloid

3. asphyxiation

4. collagenous

5. sphygmic

6. collage

## Page 17

1. d    cryophilic

2. a    crystalline

3. b    cryoscopy

4. c    crystallize

5. f    cryogenics

6. e    cryotherapy

1. cryophilic

2. crystallize

3. cryogenics

4. crystalline

5. cryotherapy

6. cryoscopy

## Page 18

1. e    dactylology

2. f    zygodactyl

3. a    dactylogram

4. b    dactylioglyph

5. d    pterodactyl

6. c    dactyloscopy

1. dactylioglyph

2. dactylogram

3. dactyloscopy

4. dactylology

5. zygodactyl

6. pterodactyl

## Page 19

1. a    echolocation

2. d    echocardiogram

3. e    echoic

4. b    echolalia

5. c    anechoic

1. anechoic

2. echolocation

3. echolalia

4. echoic

5. echocardiogram

**Page 20**

1. d   lithosphere
2. f   Paleolithic
3. a   Eoanthropus
4. b   eolith
5. c   lithography
6. e   eocene

1. eolith
2. lithography
3. Paleolithic
4. Eoanthropus
5. lithosphere
6. Eocene

**Page 21**

1. d   ergometer
2. f   metallurgy
3. a   energize
4. g   ergophobia
5. b   pyrometallurgy
6. e   ergonomics
7. c   ergogenic

1. energize
2. ergonomics
3. ergogenic
4. pyrometallurgy
5. ergometer
6. ergophobia
7. metallurgy

**Page 22**

1. c   peptic
2. e   eucalyptus
3. b   dyspepsia
4. f   peptide
5. d   eupepsia
6. a   euphoria

1. euphoria
2. peptide
3. peptic
4. dyspepsia
5. eupepsia
6. eucalyptus

**Page 23**

1. g   hypertrophy
2. f   felicity
3. a   atrophy
4. e   infelicitous
5. c   dystrophy
6. d   felicitation
7. b   trophic

1. felicity
2. hypertrophy
3. atrophy
4. infelicitous
5. dystrophy
6. felicitation
7. trophic

**Page 24**

1. b   affluence
2. a   fluctuation
3. e   fluency
4. f   influential
5. d   influx
6. c   reflux
7. g   effluent

1. influx
2. effluent
3. affluence
4. fluctuation
5. influential
6. fluency
7. reflux

**Page 25**

1. d   somnambulist
2. e   foliose
3. f   somniferous
4. b   exfoliate
5. a   insomniac
6. c   foliage

1. insomniac
2. exfoliate
3. somnambulist
4. foliose
5. foliage
6. somniferous

**Page 26**

1. d   glaciarium
2. f   glaciology
3. g   deglaciation
4. a   glacier
5. c   fluvioglacial
6. b   glaciologist
7. e   glaciation

1. glacier
2. glaciologist, glaciation
3. glaciarium
4. deglaciation, fluvioglacial
5. glaciology

**Page 27**

1. c   polyglot
2. a   glossary
3. d   glossitis
4. e   epiglottis
5. b   glossolalia

1. glossolalia
2. polyglot

3. glossary

4. epiglottis

5. glossitis

**Page 28**

1. c    tumultuous

2. f    congregation

3. g    gregarious

4. e    segregate

5. a    tumorigenic

6. b    contumacious

7. d    tumescence

1. segregate

2. contumacious

3. tumultuous

4. gregarious

5. tumescence

6. congregation

7. tumorigenic

**Page 29**

1. c    stationary

2. d    hologram

3. f    holocaust

4. b    statistics

5. a    ecstasy

6. e    holistic

1. ecstasy

2. stationary

3. statistics

4. holistic

5. hologram

6. holocaust

**Page 30**

1. e    hypnotist

2. d    hypnotherapy

3. b    hypnosis

4. a    narcohypnia

5. f    hypnotic

6. c    hypnophobia

1. hypnotic

2. hypnophobia

3. hypnotist

4. hypnosis

5. narcohypnia

6. hypnotherapy

**Page 31**

1. e    ichthyolite

2. d    ichthyosis

3. c    ichthyology

4. a    ichthyosaur

5. b    ichthyofauna

1. ichthyology

2. ichthyofauna

3. ichthyolite

4. ichthyosis

5. ichthyosaur

**Page 32**

1. e    expurgate

2. d    ablution

3. f    lavatory

4. g    deluge

5. a    purge

6. b    purity

7. c    dilution

1. purge

2. lavatory

3. dilution

4. expurgate

5. ablution, purity

6. deluge

**Page 33**

1. e    magnate

2. g    magnification

3. f    magnitude

4. a    magnificence

5. b    magniloquence

6. c    magnify

7. d    magnanimous

1. magnify

2. magnitude

3. magnanimous

4. magnate

5. magnification

6. magnificence

7. magniloquence

**Page 34**

1. d    mediation

2. f    intermediary

3. c    median

4. a    mediterranean

5. e    intermediate

6. b    medieval

1. intermediary

2. medieval

3. mediation

4. intermediate

5. mediterranean

6. median

**Page 35**

1. f    melanoma

2. e    amnesia

3. g    mnemonic

4. b    cryptomnesia

5. d    amnesty

6. a    melancholy

7. c    melanin

1. cryptomnesia

2. melanin

3. melancholy
4. melanoma
5. mnemonic
6. amnesia
7. amnesty

**Page 36**
1. e  mollescent
2. f  mollusk
3. d  emollient
4. a  mollify
5. c  molluscacide
6. b  mollification
1. mollify
2. molluscacide
3. mollification
4. mollescent
5. mollusk
6. emollient

**Page 37**
1. d  narcosis
2. e  narcomania
3. a  narcotic
4. b  narcolepsy
5. c  narcosynthesis
1. narcotic
2. narcolepsy
3. narcosis
4. narcosynthesis
5. narcomania

**Page 38**
1. f  orthodontics
2. d  orthopedist
3. e  orthodox
4. b  orthotics
5. c  orthoscopic
6. a  orthography

1. orthopedist
2. orthography
3. orthodontics
4. orthoscopic
5. orthotics
6. orthodox

**Page 39**
1. e  dioxide
2. c  paroxysm
3. f  antioxidant
4. b  peroxide
5. a  oxymoron
6. d  oxygenation
1. peroxide
2. oxymoron
3. paroxysm
4. dioxide
5. oxygenation
6. antioxidant

**Page 40**
1. d  patriarchal
2. g  paternal
3. e  expatriate
4. a  patricide
5. b  paternity
6. c  repatriation
7. f  patrimony
1. paternity
2. expatriate
3. patricide
4. paternal
5. repatriation
6. patrimony
7. patriarchal

**Page 41**
1. e  pensive

2. c  suspension
3. f  pendant
4. a  impending
5. b  append
6. d  pendulous
7. g  appendage
1. append
2. impending
3. pensive
4. pendulous
5. appendage
6. pendant
7. suspension

**Page 42**
1. e  petroleum
2. a  petroglyph
3. d  petrology
4. f  petrographic
5. b  petrify
6. c  petroliferous
1. pertrify
2. petrographic
3. petroliferous
4. petroleum
5. petrology
6. petroglyph

**Page 43**
1. d  esophagotomy
2. f  ichthyophagous
3. e  xerophagy
4. g  sarcophagus
5. c  anthropophagous
6. a  esophagus
7. b  phyllophagous
1. anthropophagous
2. phyllophagous

3. sarcophagus

4. esophagotomy

5. ichthyophagous

6. xerophagy

7. esophagus

**Page 44**

1. g  phys**iology**

2. e  phys**ic**ist

3. a  meta**phys**ics

4. f  phys**ician**

5. c  phys**ics**

6. b  phys**ical**ly

7. d  phys**ical**

1. physician

2. physical

3. physics

4. physiology

5. metaphysics

6. physicist

7. physically

**Page 45**

1. g  phyto**phagous**

2. f  phyto**logy**

3. a  phyto**chrome**

4. e  cryo**phyte**

5. b  phyto**morph**ic

6. c  phyto**therapy**

7. d  phyto**pathogen**

1. phytomorphic

2. phytotherapy

3. phytopathogen

4. phytology

5. phytophagous

6. cryophyte

7. phytochrome

**Page 46**

1. e  pla**cid**

2. a  pla**cate**

3. d  impla**cable**

4. f  pla**cebo**

5. c  compla**cent**

6. b  pla**cid**ity

1. implacable

2. complacent

3. placid

4. placate

5. placidity

6. placebo

**Page 47**

1. e  post**pon**e**ment**

2. c  op**pon**ent

3. f  com**pon**ent

4. a  pro**pon**ent

5. b  post**pon**e

6. d  ex**pon**ential

1. proponent

2. postpone

3. exponential

4. postponement

5. opponent

6. component

**Page 48**

1. d  brachy**pter**ous

2. a  **pter**osaur

3. e  **pter**ygoid

4. b  a**pter**ygial

5. c  **pter**idology

1. brachypterous

2. pteridology

3. apterygial

4. pterosaur

5. pterygoid

**Page 49**

1. c  pyreto**therapy**

2. e  a**pyret**ic

3. d  pyro**gen**ic

4. a  anti**pyret**ic

5. b  pyreto**typh**osis

1. antipyretic

2. pyretotyphosis

3. apyretic

4. pyretotherapy

5. pyrogenic

**Page 50**

1. e  con**sequ**ence

2. d  pro**secu**te

3. b  ob**sequ**ious

4. a  non **sequ**itur

5. g  per**secu**te

6. f  **sequ**ential

7. c  sub**sequ**ent

1. sequential

2. non sequitur

3. consequence

4. prosecute

5. persecute

6. obsequious

7. subsequent

**Page 51**

1. c  de**sicc**ation

2. d  de**sicc**ant

3. e  **sicc**ative

4. a  de**sicc**ate

5. b  demi-**sec**

1. siccative

2. demi-sec

3. desiccation

4. desiccate

5. desiccant

**Page 52**

1. g    selenosis

2. f    selenographer

3. e    selenodont

4. a    selenology

5. d    selenocentric

6. b    selenium

7. c    selenoscope

1. selenodont

2. selenium

3. selenocentric

4. selenosis

5. selenoscope

6. selenographer

7. selenology

**Page 53**

1. c    insurgent

2. d    traumatic

3. f    resurgence

4. e    traumatize

5. b    insurrection

6. a    post-traumatic

1. insurrection

2. traumatic

3. insurgent

4. resurgence

5. post-traumatic

6. traumatize

**Page 54**

1. e    tachistoscope

2. c    tachyon

3. f    tachymeter

4. a    tachycardia

5. b    tachygraphy

6. d    tachyphrasia

1. tachyon

2. tachygraphy

3. tachyphrasia

4. tachistoscope

5. tachycardia

6. tachymeter

**Page 55**

1. d    tenable

2. e    detention

3. a    tenure

4. f    tenacious

5. b    retentive

6. c    untenable

1. retentive

2. tenure

3. untenable

4. tenable

5. detention

6. tenacious

**Page 56**

1. c    epitome

2. e    anatomy

3. f    appendectomy

4. a    tmesis

5. b    atomize

6. d    microtome

1. appendectomy

2. atomize

3. microtome

4. anatomy

5. epitome

6. tmesis

**Page 57**

1. b    protrusive

2. e    intrude

3. d    protrude

4. c    extrusion

5. a    unobtrusive

6. f    intrusion

1. extrusion

2. protrude

3. intrude

4. unobtrusive

5. intrusion

6. protrusive

**Page 58**

1. g    vermivorous

2. e    vermicide

3. a    vermiphobia

4. b    vermin

5. c    vermicelli

6. f    verminous

7. d    vermifugal

1. vermicelli

2. vermin

3. verminous

4. vermiphobia

5. vermivorous

6. vermifugal

7. vermicide

**Page 59**

1. c    viscous

2. e    viscosity

3. a    viscometer

4. b    viscidly

5. d    viscoelasticity

1. viscidly

2. viscoelasticity

3. viscous

4. viscometer

5. viscosity

**Page 60**

1. d  xerography
2. e  xerothermic
3. f  xerophyte
4. a  xeroderma
5. c  xerophthalmia
6. b  xerographic

1. xerophthalmia
2. xerographic
3. xerothermic
4. xeroderma
5. xerography
6. xerophyte

**Page 61**

1. b  xylose
2. e  xylology
3. f  xylographer
4. a  xyloid
5. d  xylophagous
6. c  xylophone

1. xyloid
2. xylophone
3. xylology
4. xylophagous
5. xylose
6. xylographer

**Extension Worksheets**

**Worksheet One, p. 62**

1. h
2. j
3. f
4. g
5. i
6. a

7. b
8. d
9. c
10. e

**Worksheet Two, p. 63**

1. metamorphosis
2. incantation
3. helianthus
4. acoustic
5. antithesis
6. anesthetic
7. combustion
8. agoraphobia
9. anethesia
10. Platyrrhine

**Worksheet Three, p. 64**

1. platypus (2nd)
2. cinerary (1st)
3. anesthekinesia (3rd)
4. anemotropism (2nd)
5. cephalothorax (3rd)
6. hieroglyphics (1st)
7. chrysanthemum (2nd)
8. turbidity (2nd)
9. isobaric (3rd)
10. orthodox (1st)

**Worksheet Four, p. 65**

1. c
2. a
3. b
4. a
5. c
6. b
7. b
8. a

9. c
10. a

**Worksheet Five, p. 66**

1. i
2. g
3. f
4. j
5. h
6. e
7. b
8. c
9. d
10. a

**Worksheet Six, p. 67**

1. Echolalia
2. Cryotherapy
3. metallurgy
4. ergophobia
5. asphyxiation
6. felicitation
7. Hypnosis
8. tumultuous
9. collage
10. gregarious

**Worksheet Seven, p. 68**

1. holistic (2nd)
2. glaciarium (1st)
3. pyrometallurgy (2nd)
4. sphygmomanometer (3rd)
5. crystallize (1st)
6. eucalyptus (3rd)
7. tumescence (2nd)
8. pterodactyl (1st)
9. ergonomics (3rd)
10. Eoanthropus (2nd)

**Worksheet Eight, p. 69**

1. b
2. a
3. c
4. b
5. c
6. a
7. a
8. c
9. b
10. b

**Worksheet Nine, p. 70**

1. h
2. j
3. a
4. i
5. g
6. b
7. d
8. e
9. f
10. c

**Worksheet Ten, p. 71**

1. mollification
2. petroleum
3. ichthyosis
4. Petrology
5. Phyllophagous
6. narcolepsy
7. magnificence
8. oxymoron
9. melanin
10. antioxidant

**Worksheet Eleven, p. 72**

1. emollient (3rd)
2. medieval (1st)

3. sarcophagus (2nd)
4. ichthyofauna (3rd)
5. mnemonic (1st)
6. orthodontics (2nd)
7. narcosynthesis (2nd)
8. patriarchal (3rd)
9. esophagotomy (1st)
10. cryophyte (3rd)

**Worksheet Twelve, p. 73**

1. b
2. a
3. b
4. c
5. c
6. a
7. b
8. c
9. b
10. a

**Worksheet Thirteen, p. 74**

1. g
2. h
3. e
4. i
5. b
6. a
7. j
8. c
9. d
10. f

**Worksheet Fourteen, p. 75**

1. pyretotherapy
2. viscosity
3. xerophyte
4. obsequious
5. xylophagous

6. tenacious
7. traumatize
8. tachycardia
9. viscous
10. unobtrusive

**Worksheet Fifteen, p. 76**

1. appendectomy (2nd)
2. brachypterous (1st)
3. non sequitur (3rd)
4. selenodont (3rd)
5. pyretotyphosis (1st)
6. vermicelli (2nd)
7. xylose (1st)
8. xerophthalmia (3rd)
9. desiccant (2nd)
10. apterygial (1st)

**Worksheet Sixteen, p. 77**

1. c
2. a
3. c
4. b
5. b
6. a
7. c
8. a
9. b
10. c

**Worksheet Seventeen, p. 78**

Answers will vary. Accept complete sentences in which the given word makes sense according to its definition below:

1. **paradox:** a statement, situation, etc. that seems absurd or contradictory, but is or may be true

2. **cephalothorax:** fused head and thorax of an arachnid or higher crustacean

3. **archetype:** an original model on which something is patterned; prototype

4. **agoraphobia:** an abnormal fear of being in open or public places

5. **pterodactyl:** winged-fingered, prehistoric flying reptile

6. **ergonomics:** the scientific design of products, machines, etc. to maximize user safety, comfort, and efficiency

7. **isobaric:** showing equal pressure

8. **viscoelasticity:** being both viscous and elastic simultaneously

9. **Paleolithic:** related to the early Stone Age

10. **anesthekinesia:** loss of sensibility and motor power

**Latin Roots for Independent Study, p. 79**

(Answers will vary.)

**Greek Roots for Independent Study, p. 80**

(Answers will vary.)

**Anglo-Saxon (Old English) Roots for Independent Study, p. 81**

(Answers will vary.)

# Dictionary

## Pronunciation Key

| | | | | |
|---|---|---|---|---|
| ă | asp, fat, parrot | ə | (schwa) | |
| ā | ape, date, play | | a in ago | |
| ä | cot, cart, bank | | e in agent | |
| ə | ah, car, father | | i in sanity | |
| ĕ | elf, ten, berry | | o in comply | |
| ē | even, meet, money | | u in focus | |
| i | trip, lip, bit | ər | perhaps, murder | |
| ĭ | is, hit, mirror | ch | chin, catcher, arch | |
| ī | ice, bite, high | sh | she, cushion, dash | |
| ō | open, tone, go | th | thin, nothing, truth | |
| ô | all, horn, law | zh | azure, leisure | |
| oi | oil, joint, joy | | | |
| o͝o | took, book | ′ | primary accent | |
| o͞o | ooze, tool, crew | - | syllable separator | |
| oo | look, pull, moor | | | |
| yo͞o | use, cute, few | | | |
| ü | boot, rule | | | |
| ū | up, cut, color | | | |
| ûr | urn, fur, deter | | | |

## PEUMONOULTRAMICROSCOPICSILICOVOLCANOKONIOSIS

It isn't very likely that you'll come across this word in your reading, but it's fascinating in a silly way because it's so long. It certainly must be one of the longest words in English, though it's puzzling to know who would use it, since there is a much shorter word, *silicosis*, that means the same thing. It's an example of how scientists can make up new words from the ancient classical languages to describe almost anything. It's also an example of a practice that people who are very precise in the use of language object to—the mixing of Greek and Latin roots in the same word. Below is an analysis of the word:

- **pneumono** is from Greek **pneumon**, a lung.
- **ultra** is Latin, meaning "beyond, extreme" or "excessive, beyond the range of."
- **micro** is from Greek **micros**, small.
- **scopic** is from Greek **skopein**, to see.
- **silico** is from Latin **silex**, **silicis**, flint.
- **volcano** is from Latin **volcanus**, the god of fire, and means "thrown from a volcano."
- **koni** is from Greek **konia**, dust.
- **osis** is from the same root in Latin and Greek. It means "a condition," often a "diseased condition."

Putting all these roots together in the right order, you have a definition of the word simply from knowing the meanings of the roots: a diseased condition of the lungs caused by dust from volcanic flint so fine as to be beyond the range of an instrument which sees very small things.[1]

[1] Helene and Charlton Laird, *The Tree of Language*. London, England: 1957.

# GREEK AND LATIN PREFIXES

**a-**     Greek — away, from, not, without
**abranchiate** [ā-brăng´-kē-ĭt] lacking gills
**amnesia** [ăm-nē´-zhə] loss of the ability to remember
**amnesty** [ăm´-nĭ-stē] pardon; literally "forgetting a crime"
**amorphous** [ə-môr´-fəs] without definite form; shapeless
**apterygial** [ăp-tä-rĭj´-ē-əl] belonging to the group of animals without paired wings, fins, or limbs
**apyretic** [ā-pī-rēt´-ĭk] without fever
**asphyxiation** [ăs-fĭk-sē-ā´-shən] act or process of causing suffocation
**atomize** [ăt´-ə-mīz] to reduce to minute particles
**atrophy** [ă´-trə-fē] to waste away or to decrease in size as of a body part or tissue

**ab-**    Latin — away, from
**ablution** [ă-bloo´-shän] a washing of the body, especially as a religious ceremony

**af-**    Latin — to, toward, against
**affluence** [ăf´-loo-əns] an abundance of material wealth

**an-**    Greek — not, without
**anechoic** [ăn-ĕ-kō´-ĭk] free from echoes and reverberations
**anesthekinesia** [ăn-ĭs-thē-kĭ-nē´-zhə] loss of sensibility and motor power
**anesthesia** [ăn-ĭs-thē´-zhə] medically induced insensitivity to pain
**anesthesiologist** [ăn-ĭs-thē-zē-äl´-lə-jĭst] a doctor who specializes in administering drugs to prevent or relieve pain during surgery
**anesthetic** [ăn-ĕs-thĕt´-ĭk] a drug that causes temporary loss of bodily sensations

**ana-**   Greek — back, against
**anatomy** [ə-năt´-tə-mē] scientific study of the body and how its parts are arranged

**ant-**   Greek — against, opposite
**antagonistic** [ăn-tăg-ə-nĭst´-ĭk] contending with or opposing another; adversarial

**anti-**  Greek — against, opposite
**antioxidant** [ăn-tī-ôk´-sə-dənt] substance that counteracts oxidation
**antipyretic** [ăn-tē-pĭ-rĕt´-ĭk] drug that relieves or reduces fever
**antithesis** [ăn-tĭth´-ĭ-sĭs] exact opposite, contrast
**antithetic** [ăn-tə-thĕt-´ĭk] directly contrasting or opposite

**ap-**    Latin — to, toward, against
**append** [ə-pĕnd´] to attach; to state further
**appendage** [ə-pĕn´-dĭj] a projecting body part; a secondary attachment

**co-**    Latin — with, together
**coarctate** [cō-ärk´-tāt] pressed together; closely connected
**coarctation** [cō-ärk-tā´-shən] a narrowing or constriction

**com-**   Latin — with, together
**comfortable** [kəm´fərt-ə-bəl] more than adequate
**complacent** [kəm-plā´-sənt] overly pleased with oneself or one's situation; smug
**component** [kəm-pō´-nənt] a part of something larger

**con-**   Latin — with, together
**concussion** [kən-kŭsh´-ən] an injury to the brain, often resulting from a blow to the head
**congregation** [kŏn-grĭ-gā´-shən] a group of people or things gathered together; gathering
**consequence** [kōn´-sə-kwĕns] the effect, result, or outcome of something occurring earlier
**contumacious** [kän-tü-mā´-shəs] willfully obstinate

**de-**    Latin — from, away, down, apart, not

**deglaciation** [dē-glā-sē-ā´-shən] the gradual melting away of a glacier from the surface of a landmass

**deluge** [dĕl´-yo͞oj] overwhelming, flood-like rush

**desiccant** [dĕs´-ə-kənt] a substance that promotes drying

**desiccate** [dĕs´-ə-kāt] to dry completely; to deprive of moisture

**desiccation** [dĕs-ə-kā´-shən] the process of extracting moisture

**detention** [dĭ-ten´-shən] the act of detaining or holding back

**demi-**    Latin — half

**demi-sec** [dĕm´-ē-sĕk] half-dry; semi-dry

**des-**    Latin —from, away, down, apart, not

**descant** [dĕs´-kănt] high melody above the main melody

**di-**    Greek — two

**dimorphic** [dī-môr´-fĭk] occurring or existing in two different forms

**dioxide** [dī-ŏk´-sīd] an oxide containing two atoms of oxygen in the molecule

**di-**    Latin — apart, away, not

**dilution** [dī-lo͞o´-shən] something watered down; less concentrated

**dis-**    Latin — apart, opposite of

**disturbance** [dĭ-stûr´-bəns] an interruption of a state of peace or quiet

**dys-**    Greek — bad, badly

**dyspepsia** [dĭs-pĕp´-sē-ə] indigestion

**dystrophy** [dĭs´-trə-fē] any degenerative disorder resulting from inadequate or faulty nutrition

**e-**    Latin — out, away, from

**emollient** [ə-mŏl´-yənt] something that has a softening or soothing effect

**ec-**    Greek — out

**ecstasy** [ĕk´-stə-sē] a state beyond reason and self-control; overwhelming emotion

**ef-**    Latin — out

**effluent** [ĕf´-lo͞o-ənt] flowing outward or forward

**en-**    Latin — in, into

**encephalitis** [ĕn-sĕf-ə-lī´-tĭs] inflammation of the brain

**energize** [ĕn´-ər-jīz] make active

**epi-**    Greek — on, outside

**epiglottis** [ĕp-ə-glôt´-əs] a small flap at the back of the tongue that covers the windpipe during swallowing

**epitome** [ĭ-pĭt´-ə-mē] a summary or typical example of something

**eu-**    Greek — good, well

**eucalyptus** [yo͞o-kə-lĭp´-təs] Australian evergreen tree with rigid leaves and protected flowers and having medicinal and industrial value

**eupepsia** [yo͞o-pĕp´-sē-ə] good digestion

**euphoria** [yo͞o-fōr´-ē-ə] feeling of great joy, excitement, or well-being, almost to the point of exaggeration

**ex-**    Latin — out, away, from

**exasperation** [ĭg-zăs-pə-rā´-shən] annoyance and frustration

**exculpate** [ĕks-kŭl´-pāt] to clear from alleged fault or guilt; to free from blame

**exfoliate** [ĕks-fō´-lē-āt] flake or peel off

**expatriate** [ĕks-pā´-trē-āt] someone who no longer lives in his or her own country

**exponential** [ĕk-spō-nĕn´-shəl] characterized by an extremely rapid increase

**expurgate** [ĕks´-pər-gāt] to edit, to censor

**extrusion** [ĕk-stro͞o´-zhən] the action of squeezing something out by pressure

**hyper-**    Greek — over, above

**hypertrophy** [hī-pûr´-trə-fē] excessive growth or enlargement of a body part or organ

**im-**  Latin — in, into; not

**impending** [ĭm-pĕn´-dĭng] that is about to occur; imminent

**implacable** [ĭm-plă´-kə-bəl] not capable of being appeased or pacified

**in-**  Latin — in, into; not

**incantation** [ĭn-kăn-tā´-shən] the chanting of supposedly magic words

**incinerator** [ĭn-sĭn´-ə-rā-tər] a furnace for burning waste under controlled conditions

**incombustible** [ĭn-kəm-bŭs´-tə-bəl] not capable of being burned

**inculpate** [ĭn-kŭl´-pāt] to incriminate; to blame

**infelicitous** [ĭn-fə-lĭs´-ĭ-təs] unsuitable; inappropriate

**influential** [ĭn-floo-ən´-shəl] having a great deal of power to change something

**influx** [ĭn´-flŭks] the arrival of a large number of people or things

**insomniac** [ĭn-sŏm´-nē-ăk] person who is unable to sleep

**insurgent** [ĭn-sür´-jənt] person involved in a rebellion against a constituted authority

**insurrection** [ĭn-sə-rĕk´-shən] a rising up against established authority

**intrude** [ĭn-trood´] to enter uninvited

**intrusion** [ĭn-troo´-zhən] a disturbance; an invasion of someone's privacy

**inter-**  Latin — between, among

**intermediary** [ĭn-tər-mē´-dē-ĕr-ē] negotiator who acts as a link between parties

**intermediate** [ĭn-tər-mē´-dē-ĭt] being or happening between two other related things, levels, or points

**iso-**  Greek — equal

**isobaric** [ī-sə-bär´-ĭk] showing equal pressure

**meta-**  Latin — beyond, change

**metamorphosis** [mĕt-ə-môr´-fə-sĕs] a complete change of character, appearance, condition, etc.

**metaphysics** [mĕt-ĭ-fĕz´-ĭks] a branch of philosophy dealing with the nature of reality

**non-**  Latin — not

**non sequitur** [nŏ-sĕk´-wĭ-toor] a remark having no bearing on what has just been said

**ob-**  Latin — to, toward, against

**obsequious** [ŏb-sē´-kwē-əs] overly eager to please or obey

**unobtrusive** [ŭn´-əb-troo´-sĭv] inconspicuous; not standing out

**op-**  Latin — against

**opponent** [ə-pō´-nənt] one who takes an opposite position; rival

**par-**  Greek — beside, variation

**paroxysm** [păr-ək´-sĭz-əm] a sudden and uncontrollable expression of emotion

**para-**  Greek — beside, variation

**paradox** [pār´-ə-dŏks] a statement, situation, etc. that seems absurd or contradictory, but is or may be true

**per-**  Latin — through, very

**percussion** [pər-kŭsh´-ən] the group of instruments that produces sound by being struck, such as drums, cymbals, and tambourines

**peroxide** [pə-rŏk´-sīd] an oxide containing a relatively high proportion of oxygen

**persecute** [pûr´-sä-kyoot] to oppress; to pester continually

**perturb** [pər-tûrb] to disturb greatly; to upset

**repercussions** [rē-pər-kə´-shəns] the effects, often indirect or remote, of some event or action

**post-**  Latin — after

**postpone** [pōst-pōn´] to put something off until a later time; delay

**postponement** [pōst-pōn´-mənt] the act of putting something off to a future time

**post-traumatic** [pōst-trə-măt´-ĭk] occurring as a result of or after injury

**pre-**      Latin — before
             **precinct** [prē´-sǐngkt] a part of a
             territory with definite bounds

**pro-**     Latin — for, before, forward
             **proponent** [prō-pō´-nənt] one
             who argues in favor of something;
             advocate
             **prosecute** [prǒs´-ə-kyōōt] to take
             legal action and bring someone
             before a court
             **protrude** [prō-trōōd´] to bulge or
             extend forward
             **protrusive** [prō-tōō´-sǐv] jutting or
             thrusting forward

**re-**      Latin — back, again
             **recant** [rē-kǎnt´] to withdraw
             something previously said
             **reflux** [rē´-flŭks] a backward flow
             **repatriation** [rē-pā-trē-ā´-shən] the
             act of returning to one's country of
             origin
             **repercussions** [rē-pər-kush´-əns] the
             effects, often indirect or remote, of
             some event or action
             **resurgence** [rē-sür´-jəns] a rising
             again into life, activity, prominence
             **retentive** [rǐ-těn´-tǐv] tending to
             retain or hold on to

**se-**      Latin — apart, aside
             **segregate** [sěg´-rǐ-gāt] to set apart
             from the rest or from each other

**sub-**     Latin — under, below
             **subsequent** [sŭb´-sə-kwənt]
             happening or existing after; later

**suc-**     Latin — under, below
             **succinct** [sək-sǐngkt´] expressed in
             few words; concise

**sus-**     Latin — up
             **suspension** [sə-spěn´-shən] an
             interruption; literally, "to be left
             hanging"

**syn-**     Greek — with, together
             **narcosynthesis** [när-kō-sǐn´-thə-sǐs]
             a treatment of neurosis, requiring a
             patient to be under the influence of a
             hypnotic drug
             **synthesize** [sǐn´-thə-sīz] combine so
             as to form a more complex product,
             etc.

**un -**     Old English — not
             **unobtrusive** [ŭn-əb-trōō´-sǐv]
             inconspicuous; not standing out
             **untenable** [ən-těn´-ə-bəl] not able to
             be defended or justified

# GREEK AND LATIN ROOTS

**acou**  Greek — hear
**acoumeter** [ă´-ko͞o-mē-tər] instrument which measures the acuteness of hearing (Physics)
**acoustic** [ə-ko͞o´-stĭk] related to hearing or to sound as it is heard

**aesth**  Greek — feeling, perception, sensation
**aesthete** [ĕs´-thēt] one who has or affects artistic perception or appreciation of beauty
**aesthetic** [ĕs-thĕt´-ĭk] relating to the enjoyment or study of beauty

**agon**  Greek — struggle
**agony** [āg´-ə-nē] an intense feeling of suffering
**antagonistic** [ăn-tăg-ə-nĭst´-ĭk] contending with or opposing another; adversarial
**protagonist** [prō-tăg´-ə-nĭst] key figure in a contest or dispute; main character in a novel

**agora**  Greek — market-place, assembly
**agora** [ă-gər´-ə] a gathering place
**agoraphobia** [ăg-ə-rə-fō´-bē-ə] an abnormal fear of being in open or public places

**ambul**  Latin — walk
**somnambulist** [sŏm-năm´-byə-lĭst] sleepwalker

**anemo**  [combining form] Greek — wind
**anemology** [ăn-ə-mŏl´-ə-jē] the study of the movements of the winds
**anemometer** [ăn-ə-mŏm´-ə-tər] an instrument for measuring the force or speed of the wind; wind gauge
**anemophilous** [ăn-ə-mŏf´-ə-ləs] pollinated by the wind
**anemotropism** [ăn-ə-mŏ-trə´-pĭz-əm] orientation in response to air currents

**anim**  Latin — spirit, life
**magnanimous** [măg-năn´-ə-məs] generous, noble, and understanding in spirit

**anth**  Greek — flower
**anther** [ăn´-thər] the part of a flower that contains pollen
**chrysanthemum** [krĭ-săn´-thə-məm] any of a large group of plants with bright yellow, red, or white showy flowers that bloom in late summer or fall
**helianthus** [hē-lē-ăn´-thəs] tall yellow-flowered perennial related to the sunflower

**antho**  Greek — flower
**anthography** [ăn-thŏg´-rə-fē] description of flowers
**anthophagous** [ăn-thŏ´-fə-gəs] feeding on flowers
**anthophyte** [ăn´-thə-fīt] a flowering plant

**anthrop**  Greek — mankind, man
**Eoanthropus** [ē-ō-ăn´-thrō-pəs] a genus of early man comprising only the Piltdown man; dawn man

**anthropo**  Greek — mankind, man
**anthropophagous** [ăn-thrə-pŏf´-ə-gəs] feeding on human flesh; cannibalistic

**aort**  Greek — lift, raise
**aortarctia** [ā-ôr-tărk´-shə] narrowing of the aorta

**appendec**  [combining form] Greek — supplement, appendage
**appendectomy** [ăp-ən-dĕk´-tə-mē] the surgical removal of the appendix

**arch**  Greek — first, chief, rule
**hierarch** [hī´-ə-rärk] a religious leader in a position of authority

**hierarchy** [hī ´-ə-rär-kē] a system in which people or things are arranged according to their rank or status
**patriarchal** [pā-trē-är´-kəl] relating to or characteristic of a culture ruled by men

**archa**  Greek — first, chief, rule
**archaic** [är-kā´-ĭk] belonging to an earlier period; ancient

**arche**  Greek — first, chief, rule
**archetype** [är´-kĭ-tīp] an original model on which something is patterned; prototype

**arct**  Greek — to press together
**aortarctia** [ā-ôr-tärk´-shə] narrowing of the aorta
**coarctate** [cō-ärk´-tāt] pressed together; closely connected
**coarctation** [cō-ärk-tā´-shən] a narrowing or constriction

**asper**  Latin — rough
**asperity** [ă-spĕr´-ĭ-tē] harshness or severity of manner or tone
**exasperation** [ĭg-zăs-pə-rā´-shən] annoyance and frustration

**bar**  Greek — pressure, weight
**isobaric** [ī-sə-băr´-ĭk] showing equal pressure

**baro**  Greek — pressure, weight
**barometer** [bə-rŏm´-ĭ-tər] an instrument for measuring atmospheric pressure
**barometric** [băr-ə-mĕ´-trĭk] related to or indicated by a barometer

**brachy**  [combining form] Greek — short
**brachypterous** [bră-kĭp´-tər-əs] short winged

**branchi**  Greek — gill
**abranchiate** [ā-brăng´-kē-ĭt] lacking gills
**branchial** [brăng´-kē-əl] of or relating to gills

**branchio**  Greek — gill
**branchiopod** [brăng´-kē-ə-pŏd] aquatic crustacean with gills on feet

**calypt**  Greek — hidden, covered
**eucalyptus** [yoo-kə-lĭp´-təs] Australian evergreen tree with rigid leaves and protected flowers and with medicinal and industrial value

**cant**  Latin — song
**cantatrice** [kăn´-tə-trēs] female professional singer
**canticle** [kăn´-tĕ-kăl] a hymn derived from the Bible; literally a "little" song
**cantillation** [kän-tə-lā´-shən] the action of unaccompanied chanting in free rhythm
**descant** [dĕs´-kănt] high melody above the main melody
**incantation** [ĭn-kăn-tā´-shən] the chanting of supposedly magic words
**recant** [rē-kănt´] to withdraw something previously said

**card**  Greek — heart
**tachycardia** [tăk-ĭ-kär´-dē-ə] abnormally fast heartbeat

**cardio**  Greek — heart
**echocardiogram** [ĕ-kō-kär´-dē-ə-grăm] a non-invasive technique that uses ultrasound to record the functioning of the heart

**caust**  Greek — burn
**holocaust** [hŏl´-ə-kôst] total or mass destruction

**centr**  Greek — center
**selenocentric** [sə-lē-nə-sĕn´-trĭk] of or relating to the center of the moon; having the moon as center

**cephal**  Greek — head, brain
**cephalic** [sĕ-făl´-ĭk] of, or relating to the head
**encephalitis** [ĕn-sĕf-ə-lī ´-tĭs] inflammation of the brain

**cephalo**  Greek — head, brain
**cephalothorax** [sĕf-ĕ-lō-thôr´-ăks] fused head and thorax of an arachnid or higher crustacean

**chol**         Greek — bile, gall
                 **melancholy** [mĕl´-ən-kŏl-ē]
                 characterized by or expressing
                 sadness; gloomy

**chrome**       Greek — color
                 **phytochrome** [fī´-tō-krōm]
                 the pigment in green plants
                 that absorbs light and controls
                 dormancy, flowering, and the
                 germination of seeds

**chrys**        Greek — gold, yellow
                 **chrysanthemum**
                 [krĭ-săn´-thə-məm] any of a
                 large group of plants with bright
                 yellow, red, or white showy
                 flowers that bloom in late summer
                 or fall

**cinct**        Latin — surround, bind, border
                 **cincture** [sĭnct´-yēr] anything that
                 encircles, such as a belt or girdle
                 **precinct** [prē´-sĭngkt´] a part of a
                 territory with definite bounds
                 **succinct** [sək-sĭngkt´] expressed in
                 few words; concise

**cinemat**      Greek — motion, movement
                 **cinematic** [sĭn-ə-măt´-ĭk] relating
                 to the production or showing of
                 motion pictures
                 **cinematization**
                 [sĭn-ə-mə-tĭ-zā´-shən] the process
                 of adapting a novel, play, etc. for
                 film or movies

**cinemato**     Greek — motion, movement
                 **cinematography**
                 [sĭn-ə-mə-t´-ŏg´-rə-fē] the art and
                 methods of photography used in
                 film making

**ciner**        Latin — ash
                 **cinerary** [sĭn´-ə-ră-rē] containing
                 or used for ashes
                 **incinerator** [ĭn-sĭn´-ə-rā-tər] a
                 furnace for burning waste under
                 controlled conditions

**coll**         Greek — glue, gelatinous
                 **collage** [kə-läzh´] an artistic
                 composition made of various
                 materials, such as paper, cloth, or
                 wood, glued on a surface
                 **colloid** [kä´-lōid] a gelatinous
                 substance

**colla**        Greek — glue, gelatinous
                 **collagenous** [kə-lä´-jə-nəs]
                 forming or producing collagen

**combus**       Latin — burn up
                 **combustible** [kəm-bŭs´-tə-bəl]
                 able to burn easily
                 **combustion** [kəm-bŭs´-chən] act
                 or process of burning
                 **incombustible**
                 [ĭn-kəm-bŭs´-tə-bəl] not capable of
                 being burned

**crac**         Greek — government, rule
                 **hierocracy** [hī ´-ə-rŏk-rə-sē]
                 government by clergymen

**cryo**         [combining form] Greek — cold
                 **cryogenics** [krī-ō-jĕn´-ĭks] the
                 science that deals with the
                 production of extremely low
                 temperatures (Physics)
                 **cryophilic** [krī-ō-fĭl´-ĭk] capable of
                 living at low temperatures
                 **cryophyte** [krī´-ə-fīt] a plant that
                 can live or grow on snow or ice
                 **cryoscopy** [krī-ŏs´-kə-pē]
                 the science dealing with the
                 determination of the freezing
                 points of liquids
                 **cryotherapy** [krī-ō-thĕr´-ə-pē]
                 therapeutic use of cold

**crypto**       Greek — hidden
                 **cryptomnesia** [krĭp-təm-nē´-zhə]
                 a condition whereby experiences
                 are believed to be original, but are
                 actually based on memories of
                 forgotten events

**cryst**        Greek — crystal
                 **crystalline** [krĭs´-tə-lĭn] of the
                 nature of crystals
                 **crystallize** [krĭs´-tə-līz] cause to
                 form crystals

**culp**         Latin — fault, blame
                 **culpable** [kŭl´-pə-bəl] deserving
                 blame

**exculpate** [ĕks-kŭl´-pāt] to clear from alleged fault or guilt; to free from blame
**inculpate** [ĭn-kŭl´-pāt] to incriminate; to blame

**cuss**   Latin — strike, shake
**concussion** [kən-kŭsh´-ən] an injury to the brain, often resulting from a blow to the head
**percussion** [pər-kŭsh´-ən] the group of instruments that produces sound by being struck, such as drums, cymbals, and tambourines
**repercussions** [rē-pər-kŭsh´-əns] the effects, often indirect or remote, of some event or action

**dactyl**   Greek — finger, toe
**pterodactyl** [tĕr-ə-dăk´-təl] winged-fingered, prehistoric flying reptile
**zygodactyl** [zī-gō-dăk´-təl] having the toes arranged two in front and two behind

**dactylio**   Greek — finger, toe
**dactylioglyph** [dăk-tĭl´-ē-ō-glĭf] the inscription of the engraver's name on a finger ring or gem

**dactylo**   Greek — finger, toe
**dactylogram** [dăk-tĭl´-ə-grăm] a fingerprint
**dactylology** [dăk-tĭl-lä´-lə-jē] the science of communicating by using hand signs; sign language
**dactyloscopy** [dăk-tə-lŏ´-skə-pē] examination of fingerprints for purposes of identification

**derm**   Greek — skin
**xeroderma** [zîr-ō-dûr´-mə] abnormal dryness of the skin (Medical)

**dog**   Greek — opinion, praise
**dogma** [dôg´-mə] something held as an established opinion

**dont**   Latin — teeth
**orthodontics** [ôr-thə-dŏn´-tĭks] the branch of dentistry concerned

with the prevention or correction of irregularities of the teeth
**selenodont** [sə-lē´-nə-dänt] having molars with crowns formed of crescent-shaped cusps

**dox**   Greek — opinion, praise
**doxology** [dŏk-sŏl´-ə-jē] a liturgical formula of praise to God
**orthodox** [ôr´-thə-dŏks] adhering to what is commonly accepted opinion
**paradox** [păr´-ə-dŏks] a statement, situation, etc. that seems absurd or contradictory, but is or may be true

**echo**   Greek — sound
**anechoic** [ăn-ĕ-kō´-ĭk] free from echoes and reverberations
**echocardiogram** [ĕ-kō-kär´-dē-ə-grăm] a non-invasive technique that uses ultrasound to record the functioning of the heart
**echoic** [ĕ-kō´-ĭk] formed in imitation of some natural sound
**echolalia** [ĕk-ô-lā´-lē-ə] involuntary parrot-like repetition of a word or phrase just spoken by another; echoing
**echolocation** [ĕk-ō-lō-kā´-shən] a means of locating an object using an emitted sound and the reflection back from it

**elast**   Greek — expansive
**viscoelasticity** [vĭs-kō-ĭ-lăs-tĭ´-sĭ-tē] being both viscous and elastic simultaneously

**eo**   Greek — dawn, early
**Eoanthropus** [ē-ō-an´-thrō-pəs] a genus of early man comprising only the Piltdown man; dawn man
**Eocene** [ē´-ə-sēn] relating to the second epoch of the Tertiary period
**eolith** [ē´-ə-lĕth] a very early and crude stone tool

**erg**   Greek — work, power
**energize** [ĕn´-ər-jīz] to make active

**ergo**      Greek — work, power
**ergogenic** [ûr-gə-jĕn´-ĭk] increasing capacity for physical or mental labor
**ergometer** [ûr-gə´-mət-ər] a device for measuring work performance
**ergonomics** [ûr-gə-nom-´ĭks] the scientific design of products, machines, etc. to maximize user safety, comfort, and efficiency
**ergophobia** [ər-gə-fō´-bē-ə] abnormal and persistent fear of work or the workplace

**eso**       Latin — to bear, to carry
**esophagotomy** [ĭ-săf-ə-gŏt´-ə-mē] incision through the wall of the esophagus (Medical)
**esophagus** [ĭ-sŏf´-ə-gəs] the part of the digestive tract that connects the throat to the stomach (Medical)

**esth**      Greek — sensation, feeling, perception
**anesthesia** [ăn-ĭs-thē´-zhə] medically induced insensitivity to pain
**anesthetic** [ăn-ĭs-thĕt´-ĭk] a drug that causes temporary loss of bodily sensations

**esthe**     Greek — sensation, feeling, perception
**anesthekinesia** [ān-ĭs-thē-kĭ-nē´-zhə] loss of sensibility and motor power

**esthesi**   Greek — sensation, feeling, perception
**anesthesiologist** [ăn-ĭs-thē-zē-ä´-lə-jĭst] a doctor who specializes in administering drugs to prevent or relieve pain during surgery

**esthesio**  Greek — sensation, feeling, perception
**esthesiometer** [ĕs-thē-zē-öm´-ĭ-tər] an instrument used to measure tactile sensitivity

**ev**        Latin — age, time
**medieval** [mēd-ē´-vəl] relating or belonging to the Middle Ages

**fauna**     Latin — animal life
**ichthyofauna** [ĭk-thē-ō-fä´-nə] the fish of a particular region

**felic**     Latin — pleasing, happy, suitable
**felicitation** [fĭ-lĭs-ĭ-tā´-shən] an expression of pleasure at the success or good fortune of another
**felicity** [fĭ-lĭs´-ə-tē] pleasing and appropriate manner; happiness
**infelicitous** [ĭn-fə-lĭs´-ĭ-təs] unsuitable; inappropriate

**flu**       Latin — flowing
**affluence** [ăf´-lōō-ăns] an abundance of material wealth
**effluent** [ĕf´-lōō-ənt] flowing outward or forward
**fluency** [flōō´-ən-sē] effortless expression
**influential** [ĭn-flōō´-ən´-shəl] having a great deal of power to change something

**fluc**      Latin — flowing
**fluctuation** [flŭk-chōō-ā-´shən] variation in level, degree; constant change

**fluvio**    Latin — flowing
**fluvioglacial** [flōō-vē-ŏ-glā´-shəl] pertaining to streams flowing from glaciers or to the deposits made by such streams (Geology)

**flux**      Latin — flowing
**influx** [ĭn´-flŭks] the arrival of a large number of people or things
**reflux** [rē´-flŭks] a backward flow

**foli**      Latin — leaf
**exfoliate** [ĕks-fō´-lē-āt] flake or peel off
**foliage** [fō´-l-ē-ĭj] leaves, as of a plant or tree
**foliose** [fō´-lē-ōs] covered with leaves; leafy

**fort**      Latin — strong
**comfortable** [kəm´-fərt-ə-bəl] more than adequate

**fortification** [fōrt-ə-fə-kā´-shən] the act or process of strengthening
**fortify** [fôr´-tə-fī] to strengthen, especially in order to protect
**fortitude** [fôr´-tə-tüd] courage and strength in bearing pain or trouble

**fug**  Latin — flee
**vermifugal** [vûr-mə-fyŏŏ´-gəl] tending to expel worms

**gen**  Greek — cause, birth, race, produce
**collagenous** [kə-lä´-jə-nəs] forming or producing collagen
**cryogenics** [krī-ō-jĕn´-ĭks] the science that deals with the production of extremely low temperatures (Physics)
**ergogenic** [ûr-gə-jĕn´-ĭk] increasing capacity for physical or mental labor
**oxygenation** [ŏk-sē-jĕ-nā´-shən] the process of providing oxygen
**phytopathogen** [fī-tō-pă´-thə-jən] something that causes disease in plants
**pyrogenic** [pī-rō-jen´-ĭk] fever inducing
**tumorigenic** [tŏŏ-mər-ĭ-jĭn´-ĭk] producing or tending to produce tumors

**glac**  Latin — ice
**deglaciation** [dē-glā-sē-ā´-shən] the gradual melting away of a glacier from the surface of a landmass
**fluvioglacial** [flŏŏ-vē-ō-glā´-shəl] pertaining to streams flowing from glaciers or to the deposits made by such streams (Geology)
**glaciarium** [glā-sē-ăr´-ē-ŭm] a skating rink with a floor of artificial ice
**glaciation** [glā-sē-ā´-shən] the process of being covered or covering with masses of ice
**glacier** [glā´-shər] a slowly moving mass of ice
**glaciologist** [glā-sē-ŏl´-ə-jĭst] expert in the formation, movements, etc. of glaciers

**glaciology** [glā-sē-ŏl´-ə-jē] the scientific study of the nature, formation, and movement of glaciers

**gloss**  Greek — language, tongue
**glossary** [glôs´-ə-rē] an alphabetical list of specialized words with their definitions, usually at the back of a book
**glossitis** [glö-sī´-təs] inflammation of the tongue

**glosso**  Greek — language, tongue
**glossolalia** [glös-ŏ-lā´-lē-ə] repetitive non-meaningful speech

**glot**  Greek — language, tongue
**polyglot** [pŏl´-ē-glŏt] a person who speaks several different languages

**glott**  Greek — language, tongue
**epiglottis** [ĕp-ə-glŏt´-əs] a small flap at the back of the tongue that covers the windpipe during swallowing

**glyph**  Greek — carve
**dactylioglyph** [dăk-tĭl´-ē-ō-glĭf] the inscription of the engraver's name on a finger ring or gem
**hieroglyphics** [hī-rə-glĭf´-ĭks] the picture script of the ancient Egyptian priesthood
**petroglyph** [pĕt´-rə-glĭf] ancient carving or inscription on rock

**gram**  Greek — write, written
**dactylogram** [dăk-tĭl´-ə-grăm] a finger print
**echocardiogram** [ĕ-kō-kär´-dē-ə-grăm] a non-invasive technique that uses ultrasound to record the functioning of the heart
**hologram** [hŏl´-ə-grăm] 3-dimensional photographical image

**graph**  Greek — write, written
**anthography** [ăn-thŏg´-rə-fē] description of flowers

**cinematography** [sĭn-ə-mə-tŏg´-rə-fē] the art and methods of photography used in film making
**lithography** [lĭ-thŏg´-rə-fē] the process or method of printing from a metal or stone surface
**orthography** [ôr-thŏg´-rə-fē] spelling in accord with accepted usage
**petrographic** [pĕt-rə-grăf´-ĭk] related to the systematic description and classification of rocks using microscopic examination
**selenographer** [sĕl-lə-nŏg´-rə-fûr] expert in mapping the physical features of the moon
**tachygraphy** [tă-kĭg´-rə-fē] the art or technique of rapid writing or shorthand
**xerographic** [zĭ´-ə-grăf´-ĭk] related to electrophotography or dry photocopying
**xerography** [zĭ-rŏg´-rə-fē] method of dry photocopying in which the image is transferred by using the forces of electric charges
**xylographer** [zī-lŏg´-rə-fər] one who is skilled in artistic wood carving

**greg**  Latin — herd, flock
**congregation** [kŏn-grĭ-gā´-shən] a group of people or things gathered together; gathering
**gregarious** [grĭ-găr´-ē-əs] fond of company; sociable
**segregate** [sĕg´-rĭ-gāt] to set apart from the rest or from each other

**heli**  Greek — sun
**helianthus** [hē´-lē-an-thəs] tall yellow-flowered perennial related to the sunflower

**helminth**  Greek — worm
**platyhelminth** [plăt-ē-hĕl´-mĭnth] parasitic or free-living worms having a flattened body

**hier**  Greek — sacred
**hierarch** [hī´-ə-rärk] a religious leader in a position of authority
**hierarchy** [hī´-ə-rär-kē] a system in which people or things are arranged according to their rank or status

**hiero**  Greek — sacred
**hierocracy** [hī´-ə-rŏk-rə-sē] government by clergymen
**hieroglyphics** [hī-rə-glĭf´-ĭks] the picture script of the ancient Egyptian priesthood

**hol**  Greek — entire, whole
**holistic** [hō-lĭs´-tĭk] involving all of something

**holo**  Greek — entire, whole
**holocaust** [hŏl´-ə-kost] total or mass destruction
**hologram** [hŏl-ə-grăm´] 3-dimensional photographical image

**hypn**  [coming form] Greek — sleep
**hypnosis** [hĭp´-nō-sĭs] a state that resembles sleep but is induced by suggestion
**narcohypnia** [när-kō-hĭp´-nē-ə] numbness experienced upon awakening

**hypno**  [combining form] Greek — sleep
**hypnophobia** [hĭp-nə-fō´-bē-ə] an abnormal fear of falling asleep
**hypnotherapy** [hĭp-nō-thĕr´-ə-pē] the use of hypnosis in treating illness or emotional problems
**hypnotic** [hĭp-nŏt´-ĭk] relating to or involving sleep or hypnosis
**hypnotist** [hĭp´-nə-tĭst] a person who uses hypnosis as a form of treatment

**ichthy**  Greek — fish
**ichthyosis** [ĭk-thē´-ō-sĭs] congenital disease in which the skin is fishlike (dry and scaly) (Medical)

**ichthyo**    Greek — fish
**ichthyofauna** [ĭk-thē-ō-fä´-nə] the fish of a particular region
**ichthyolite** [ĭk-thē´-ō-līt] a fossil fish or fragment of a fish
**ichthyology** [ĭk-thē-ŏl´-ə-jē] the study of fishes
**ichthyophagous** [ik-thē-ä´-fə-gəs] fish-eating
**ichthyosaur** [ik´-thĕ-ə-sôr] an extinct variety of fishlike marine reptiles of the Mesozoic period

**kin**    Greek — motion
**anesthekinesia** [ān-ĭs-the-ō-kĭ-nē´-zhə] loss of sensibility and motor power
**kinesiology** [kə-nē-sē-ŏl´-ə-jē] the study of human musculoskeletal movement
**kinesthesis** [kĭn-ĭs-the-ē´-sĭs] the ability to feel movements of the limbs and body
**kinetic** [kə-nĕ´-tĭk] related to movement

**lal**    Greek — talk, babble
**echolalia** [ĕk-ō-lā´-lē-ə] involuntary parrot-like repetition of a word or phrase just spoken by another, echoing
**glossolalia** [glös-ō-lā´-lē-ə] repetitive non-meaningful speech

**lav**    Latin — wash, bathe
**lavatory** [lăv´-ə-tôr-ē] a room equipped with toilette facilities

**leps**    Latin — take, seize
**narcolepsy** [när´-kō-lĕp-sē] a sleep disorder characterized by sudden and uncontrollable episodes of deep sleep

**litho**    Greek — stone
**lithography** [lĭ-thŏg´-rə-fē] the process or method of printing from a metal or stone surface
**lithosphere** [lĭth´-ə-sfîr] the outer part of the solid earth composed of rock

**locat**    Latin — place
**echolocation** [ĕk-ō-lō-kā´-shən] a means of locating an object

using an emitted sound and the reflection back from it

**loqu**    Latin — speak
**magniloquence** [măg-nĭl´-ə-kwəns] excessive use of verbal ornamentation; pompous discourse

**lu**    Latin — wash, bathe
**ablution** [ă-bloo´-shən] a washing of the body, especially as a religious ceremony
**dilution** [dī-loo´-shən] something watered down; less concentrated

**luge**    Latin — wash, bathe
**deluge** [dĕl´-yooj] an overwhelming, flood-like rush

**magn**    Latin — great, large
**magnanimous** [măg-năn´-ə-məs] generous, noble, and understanding in spirit
**magnate** [măg´-nāt] a person of high rank, power, influence, etc. in a specific field

**magni**    Latin — great, large
**magnification** [măg-nĕ-fī-kā´-shən] the process of making something look bigger than it really is
**magnificence** [măg-nĭ´-fĭ-səns] splendid or grand in size or appearance
**magnify** [măg´-nĭ-fī] to increase in size; enlarge
**magniloquence** [măg-nĭl´-ə-kwəns] excessive use of verbal ornamentation; pompous discourse
**magnitude** [măg´-nĭ-tüd] greatness of size, volume, or extent

**mano**    Greek — gas
**sphygmomanometer** [sfĭg-mō-mə-nŏm´-ə-tər] an instrument which measures blood pressure in the arteries

**mania**  Greek — intense craving
**narcomania** [när-kō-mān′-ē-ə] abnormal craving for a drug to deaden pain

**medi**  Latin — half, middle, halfway between
**intermediary** [ĭn-tər′-mē-dē-ĕr-ē] a negotiator who acts as a link between parties
**intermediate** [ĭn-tər-mē′-dē-ĭt] being or happening between two other related things, levels, or points
**median** [mē′-dē-ən] related to or situated in the middle
**mediation** [mē-dē-ā-′shən] the process of resolving differences
**medieval** [mēd-ē′-vəl] relating or belonging to the Middle Ages
**mediterranean** [měd′-ĭ-tə-rā-nē-ən] enclosed or nearly enclosed with land

**melan**  Greek — black, dark
**melancholy** [měl-ən-kŏl′-ē] characterized by or expressing sadness; gloomy
**melanin** [měl′-ə-nĭn] a brownish-black pigment found in skin
**melanoma** [měl-ə-nō′-mə] a type of skin cancer that appears as a dark mark or growth on the skin

**metall**  Greek —metal, mine
**metallurgy** [mět′-l-ûr-jē] the science and technology of extracting metals from their ores
**pyrometallurgy** [pī′-rō-mět-l-ûr-jē] chemical metallurgy that depends on heat action

**meter**  Greek — measure
**acoumeter** [ă′-kōō-mē-tər] instrument which measures the acuteness of hearing (Physics)
**anemometer** [ăn-ə-mŏm′-ə-tər] an instrument for measuring the force or speed of the wind; wind gauge
**barometer** [bə-rŏm′-ĭ-tər] an instrument for measuring atmospheric pressure

**ergometer** [ûr-gə′-mət-ər] a device for measuring work performance
**esthesiometer** [ĕs-thē-zē-öm′-ĕ-tər] an instrument used to measure tactile sensitivity
**sphygmomanometer** [sfĭg-mō-mə-nŏm′-ə-tər] an instrument which measures blood pressure in the arteries
**tachymeter** [tă-kŏm′-ĕ-tər] device for measuring speed of rotation
**viscometer** [vĭ-skŏm′-ĭ-tər] instrument for measuring viscosity

**metr**  Greek — measure
**barometric** [băr-ə-mi′-trĭk] related to or indicated by a barometer

**micro**  [combining form] Greek — small
**microtome** [mī′-krə-tōm] scientific instrument that cuts thin slices of biological tissues for microscopic examination

**mnem**  Greek — memory, remember
**mnemonic** [nĭ-mŏn′-ĭk] a short rhyme, phrase, etc. for making information easier to remember

**mnes**  Greek — remember, memory
**amnesia** [ăm-nē′-zhə] loss of the ability to remember
**amnesty** [ăm′-nĭ-stē] pardon; literally "forgetting a crime"
**cryptomnesia** [krĕp-təm-nē′-zhə] a condition whereby experiences are believed to be original, but are actually based on memories of forgotten events

**moll**  Latin — soft
**emollient** [ə-mŏl′-yənt] something that has a softening or soothing effect
**mollescent** [mə-lĕ′-sənt] softening or tending to soften
**mollification** [mŏl-ə-fĭ-kā′-shən] appeasement
**mollify** [mŏl′-ə-fī] to soothe the temper of; appease; soften
**molluscacide** [mə-lə′-skə-sīd] a chemical pesticide used to kill mollusks

**mollusk**   Latin — soft
**mollusk** [mōl´-ăsk] an invertebrate animal having a soft unsegmented body usually enclosed in a shell

**mor**   Latin — stupid
**oxymoron** [ŏk-se-môr´-ŏn] a combination of contradictory or incongruous words

**morph**   Greek — form
**amorphous** [ə-môr´-fəs] without definite form; shapeless
**dimorphic** [dī-môr´-fĭk] occurring or existing in two different forms
**metamorphosis** [mĕt-ə-môr´-fə-sĕs] a complete change of character, appearance, condition, etc.
**morphology** [môr-fŏl´-ə-jē] the study of the form and structure of organisms
**phytomorphic** [fī-tō-môr´-fĭk] having attributes of a plant

**narc**   Greek — numbness, stupor
**narcosis** [när-kō´-sĭs] a state of stupor or greatly reduced activity produced by a drug or other element

**narco**   [combining form] Greek — numbness, stupor
**narcolepsy** [när´-kō-lĕp-sē] a sleep disorder characterized by sudden and uncontrollable episodes of deep sleep
**narcohypnia** [när-kō-hĭp´-nē-ə] numbness experienced upon awakening
**narcomania** [när-kō-mān´-ē-ə] abnormal craving for a drug to deaden pain
**narcosynthesis** [när-kō-sĭn´-thə-sĭs] a treatment of neurosis, requiring a patient to be under the influence of a hypnotic drug
**narcotic** [när-kŏ´-tĕk] a drug used to relieve pain and induce sleep

**nom**   Greek — name, law, custom, order
**ergonomics** [ûr-gə-nôm´-ĭks] the scientific design of products, machines, etc. to maximize user safety, comfort, and efficiency

**ophthalm**   Greek — eye
**xerophthalmia** [zĭr-əf-thăl´-mē-ə] excessive dryness of the conjunctiva and cornea of the eye (Medical)

**ortho**   Greek — straight, right
**orthodontics** [ôr-thə-dŏn´-tĭks] the branch of dentistry concerned with the prevention or correction of irregularities of the teeth
**orthodox** [ôr´-thə-dŏks] adhering to what is commonly accepted
**orthography** [ôr-thŏg´-rə-fē] spelling in accord with accepted usage
**orthopedist** [ôr-thə-pēd´-ĭst] a specialist in correcting deformities of the skeletal system especially in children
**orthoscopic** [ôr-thō-skŏp´-ĭk] related to seeing an image in correct and normal proportion
**orthotics** [ôr-thə´-tĭks] the science that deals with the developing and fitting of medical devices

**ox**   Greek — sharp, acid, acute
**antioxidant** [ăn-tī-ŏk´-sə-dənt] substance that counteracts oxidation
**dioxide** [dī-ŏk´-sīd] an oxide containing two atoms of oxygen in the molecule
**peroxide** [pə-rŏk´-sīd] an oxide containing a relatively high proportion of oxygen

**oxy**   Greek — sharp, acid, acute
**oxygenation** [ŏk-sē-jĕ-nā´-shən] the process of providing oxygen
**oxymoron** [ŏk-sē-môr´-ŏn] a combination of contradictory or incongruous words

**oxysm**   Greek — sharp, acid, acute
**paroxysm** [păr-ək´-sĭz-əm] a sudden and uncontrollable expression of emotion

**paleo** | Greek — [combining form] ancient, old
**Paleolithic** [pā-lē-ə-lĭth´-ĭk] related to the early Stone Age

**pater** | Latin — father
**paternal** [pə-tûr´-nəl] related on the father's side
**paternity** [pə-tûr´-nə-tē] the fact or state of being a father; fatherhood

**patho** | Greek — feeling, disease
**phytopathogen** [fī-tō-pă´-thə-jən] something that causes disease in plants

**patri** | Latin — father
**expatriate** [ĕks-pā´-trē-ăt] someone who no longer lives in his or her own country
**patriarchal** [pā-trē-är´-kəl] relating to or characteristic of a culture ruled by men
**patricide** [păt´-rə-sīd] the killing of a father by his own child
**patrimony** [păt´-rə-mō-nē] an estate inherited from one's father or ancestor
**repatriation** [rē-pă-trē´-ā-shən] the act of returning to one's country of origin

**ped** | Latin — child
**orthopedist** [ôr-thə-pēd´-ĭst] a specialist in correcting deformities of the skeletal system, especially in children

**pend** | Latin — hang, weigh
**append** [ə-pĕnd´] to attach; to state further
**appendage** [ə-pĕn´-dĭj] a projecting body part; a secondary attachment
**impending** [ĭm-pĕn´-dĭng] that is about to occur; imminent
**pendant** [pĕn´-dənt] an ornamental, hanging object
**pendulous** [pĕn´-jōō-ləs] hanging loosely or swinging freely

**pens** | Latin — hang, weigh
**pensive** [pĕn´-sĭv] thoughtfully weighing an issue or problem

**suspension** [sə-spĕn´-shən] an interruption; literally, "to be left hanging"

**peps** | Greek — digest
**dyspepsia** [dĭs-pĕp´-sē-ə] indigestion
**eupepsia** [yōō-pĕp´-sē-ə] good digestion

**pept** | Greek — digest
**peptic** [pĕp´-tĭk] relating to digestion
**peptide** [pĕp´-tīd] a compound with amino bonds

**petr** | Greek — rock
**petrify** [pĕt´-trə-fī] to turn organic matter into stone

**petro** | Greek — rock
**petroglyph** [pĕt´-rə-glĭf] ancient carving or inscription on rock
**petrographic** [pĕt-rə-grăf´-ĭk] related to the systematic description and classification of rocks using microscopic examination
**petroleum** [pə-trō´-lē-əm] crude oil that occurs naturally in sedimentary rocks and consists mainly of hydrocarbons
**petroliferous** [pĕ-trə-lĭf´-ər-əs] containing or yielding petroleum
**petrology** [pə-trŏl´-ə-jē] the study of the origin, formation, and composition of rocks

**phag** | Greek — eat
**anthophagous** [ăn-thŏ-fə-gəs´] feeding on flowers
**anthropophagous** [ăn-thrə´-pŏf-ə-gəs] feeding on human flesh; cannibalistic
**esophagus** [ĭ-sŏf´-ə-gəs] the part of the digestive tract that connects the throat to the stomach (Medical)
**ichthyophagous** [ĭk-thē-ä´-fə-gəs] fish-eating
**phyllophagous** [fĭ-lŏf´-ə-gəs] feeding on leaves; leaf-eating
**phytophagous** [fī-tŏf´-ə-gəs] plant-eating; herbivorous

**sarcophagus** [sär-kŏf´-ə-gəs] an ornamental stone coffin used to decompose the flesh of the corpse within

**xerophagy** [zĭ-rof´-ə-jē] eating of dry food

**xylophagous** [zī-lŏf´-ə-gəs] feeding on wood

**phago**   Greek — eat
**esophagotomy** [ĭ-săf-ə-gŏt´-ə-mē] incision through the wall of the esophagus (Medical)

**phil**   Greek — love, loving
**anemophilous** [ăn-ə-mŏf´-ə-ləs] pollinated by the wind

**cryophilic** [krī-ō-fĭl´-ĭk] capable of living at low temperatures

**phob**   Greek — fear of
**agoraphobia** [ăg-ə-rə-fō´-bē-ə] abnormal fear of being in open or public places

**ergophobia** [ər-gə-fō´-bē-ə] abnormal and persistent fear of work or the workplace

**hypnophobia** [hĭp-nə-fō´-bē-ə] an abnormal fear of falling asleep

**vermiphobia** [vûr-mə-fō´-bē-ə] fear of worms

**phone**   Greek — sound
**xylophone** [zī´-lə-fōn] a musical instrument of flat, wooden bars of different lengths that produce notes when hit with sticks

**phor**   Greek — bear, produce
**euphoria** [yo͞o-fōr´-ē-ə] a feeling of great joy, excitement, or well-being, almost to the point of exaggeration

**phras**   Greek — speech
**tachyphrasia** [tăk-ĭ-frā´-zhə] abnormally rapid yet fluent and articulate speech

**phyll**   Greek — leaf
**phyllophagous** [fĭ-lŏf´-ə-gəs] feeding on leaves; leaf-eating

**phys**   Greek — nature, growth
**metaphysics** [mĕt-ə-fĭz´-ĭks] a branch of philosophy dealing with the nature of reality

**physical** [fĭz´-ĭ-kəl] of or relating to the body

**physically** [fĭz´-ĭ-kəl-lē] in a physical manner; in respect to the body

**physician** [fĭ-zĭsh´-ən] a person skilled in the art of healing

**physicist** [fĭz´-ə-sĭst] a scientist whose specialty is physics

**physics** [fĭz´-ĭks] related to matter and energy and their interactions

**physiology** [fĭz-ē-ŏl´-ə-jē] the branch of the biological sciences that deals with the functioning of organisms

**phyte**   Greek — plant
**anthophyte** [ăn´-thə-fīt] a flowering plant

**cryophyte** [krī´-ə-fīt] a plant that can live or grow on snow or ice

**xerophyte** [zîr´-ə-fīt] a plant structurally adapted for growth in dry conditions

**phyto**   Greek — plant
**phytochrome** [fī´-tŏ-krōm] the pigment in green plants that absorbs light and controls dormancy, flowering, and the germination of seeds

**phytology** [fī-tŏl´-ə-jē] the study of plants; botany

**phytomorphic** [fī-tō-môr´-fĭk] having attributes of a plant

**phytopathogen** [fī-tō-pă´-thə-jən] something that causes disease in plants

**phytophagous** [fī-tŏf´-ə-gəs] plant-eating; herbivorous

**phytotherapy** [fī-tō-thər´-ə-pē] the use of herbs and other plants to promote health and treat disease

**plac**   Latin — please, soothe, gentle
**complacent** [kəm-plā´-sənt] overly pleased with oneself or one's situation; smug

**implacable** [ĭm-plă´-kə-bəl] not capable of being appeased or pacified

**placate** [plā´-kāt] to soothe or mollify; appease

**placebo** [plə-sē´-bō] something done or said simply to reassure

**placid** [plăs´-ĭd] calm in nature; tranquil

**placidity** [plə-sĭd´-ĭ-tē] the quality or feeling of being calm or composed

**platy** [combining form] Greek — flat, broad

**platyhelminth** [plăt-ē-hĕl´-mĭnth] parasitic or free-living worms having a flattened body

**platypus** [plăt´-ĭ-pəs] an aquatic animal with a broad, flat bill

**platyrrhine** [plăt´-ĭ-rīn] characterized by a broad, flat nose

**pod** Greek — foot

**branchiopod** [brăng´-kē-ə-pŏd] aquatic crustacean with gills on feet

**poly** [combining form] Greek — many

**polyglot** [pŏl´-ē-glŏt] a person who speaks several different languages

**pon** Latin — place, put

**component** [kəm-pō´-nənt] a part of something larger

**exponential** [ĕk-spō-nĕn´-shəl] characterized by an extremely rapid increase

**opponent** [ə-pō´-nənt] one who takes an opposite position; rival

**proponent** [prō-pŏ´-nənt] one who argues in favor of something; advocate

**pone** Latin — place, put

**postpone** [pōst-pōn´] to put something off until a later time; delay

**postponement** [pōst-pōn´-mənt] the act of putting something off to a future time

**prot** Greek — first, ahead

**protagonist** [prĕ-tăg´-ə-nĭst] key figure in a contest or dispute; main character in a novel

**pter** Greek — wing, feather

**apterygial** [ăp-tə-rĭj´-ē-əl] belonging to the group of animals without paired wings, fins, or limbs

**brachypterous** [bră-kĭp´-tər-əs] short winged

**pteridology** [tĕr-ĕ-dŏl´-ə-jē] the branch of botany that studies ferns

**pterygoid** [tĕr´-ə-goid] like a bird's wing in form or limbs

**ptero** Greek — wing, feather

**pterodactyl** [tĕr-ə-dăk´-təl] winged-fingered, prehistoric flying reptile

**pterosaur** [tĕr´-ə-sor] extinct flying reptile

**pur** Latin — clean

**purity** [pyo͝or´-ĭ-tē] the quality or state of being clean

**purg** Latin — clean

**expurgate** [ĕks´-pər-gāt] to edit, to censor

**purge** [pûrj] to cleanse or clear

**pus** Greek — foot

**platypus** [plăt´-ĭ-pəs] an aquatic animal with a broad, flat bill

**pyret** Greek — fever

**antipyretic** [ăn-tē-pĭ-rĕt´-ĭk] drug that relieves or reduces fever

**apyretic** [ā-pī-rĕt´-ĭk] without fever

**pyreto** [combining form] Greek — fever

**pyretotherapy** [pīr-ĭ-tō-thĕr´-ə-pē] fever therapy

**pyretotyphosis** [pĭ-rə-tō-tĭ´-fō-sĭs] the delirium of fever

**pyro** [combining form] Greek — fire, heat

**pyrogenic** [pī-rō-jĕn´-ĭk] fever inducing

**pyrometallurgy** [pī-rō-mĕt´-l-ûr-jē] chemical metallurgy that depends on heat action

**rrhine** Greek — nose
**platyrrhine** [plăt´-ĭ-rīn] characterized by a broad, flat nose

**sarco** Greek — flesh
**sarcophagus** [sär-kŏf´-ə-gəs] an ornamental stone coffin used to decompose the flesh of the corpse within

**saur** Greek — lizard
**ichthyosaur** [ĭk´-thē-ə-sôr] an extinct variety of fishlike marine reptiles of the Mesozoic period
**pterosaur** [tĕr´-ə-sôr] extinct flying reptile

**scop** Greek— look, view, examine
**cryoscopy** [krī-ŏs´-kə-pē] the science dealing with the determination of the freezing points of liquid
**dactyloscopy** [dăk-tə-lŏ´-skə-pē] examination of fingerprints for purposes of identification
**orthoscopic** [ôr-thō-skōp´-ĭk] related to seeing an image in correct and normal proportion

**scope** Greek— look, view, examine
**selenoscope** [sĕ-lən´-ō-skōp] instrument for viewing the moon
**tachistoscope** [tă-kĭs´-tə-skōp] instrument for rapidly showing images on a screen to test perception

**sec** Latin— dry
**demi-sec** [dĕm´-ē-sĕk] half-dry; semi-dry

**secute** Latin — follow
**persecute** [pûr´-sə-kyo͞ot] to oppress; to pester continually
**prosecute** [prŏs´-ə-kyo͞ot] to take legal action and bring someone before a court

**selen** Greek — moon, brightness
**selenium** [sə-lə´-nē-əm] a trace mineral that has light-sensitive properties

**selenosis** [sĕ-lə-nō´-sĭs]poisoning caused by ingesting dangerously high amounts of selenium

**seleno** Greek — moon, brightness
**selenocentric** [sə-lē-nə-sĕn´-trĭk] of or relating to the center of the moon; having the moon as center
**selenodont** [sə-lē´-nə-dänt] having molars with crowns formed of crescent-shaped cusps
**selenographer** [sĕl-lə-nŏg´-rə-fûr] expert in mapping the physical features of the moon
**selenology** [sĕ-lə-nŏl´-ə-jē] the study of the origin and physical characteristics of the moon
**selenoscope** [sĕ-lən´-ō-skōp] instrument for viewing the moon

**sequ** Latin — follow
**consequence** [kŏn´-sə-kwĕns] the effect, result, or outcome of something occurring earlier
**non sequitur** [nŏn-sĕk´-wĕ-to͝or] a remark having no bearing on what has just been said
**obsequious** [ŏb-sē´-kwē-əs] overly eager to please or obey
**sequential** [sē-kwĕn´-shəl] following in regular succession without gaps
**subsequent** [sŭb´-sə-kwənt] happening or existing after; later

**sicc** Latin — dry
**desiccant** [dĕs´-ə-kənt] a substance that promotes drying
**desiccate** [dĕs´-ə-kāt] to dry completely; to deprive of moisture
**desiccation** [dĕs-ə-kā´-shən] the process of extracting moisture
**siccative** [sĭk´-ə-tĭv] causing to dry; drying

**somn** Latin — sleep
**insomniac** [ĭn-sŏm´-nē-ăk] person who is unable to sleep
**somnambulist** [sŏm-năm´-byə-lĭst] sleepwalker
**somniferous** [sŏm-nĭf´-ər-əs] sleep inducing

| | | | |
|---|---|---|---|
| **sphere** | Greek — ball<br>**lithosphere** [lĭth´-ə-sfir] the outer part of the solid earth composed of rock | | **tachyon** [tăk´-ē-ŏn] a hypothetical subatomic particle that can travel faster than the speed of light<br>**tachyphrasia** [tăk-ĭ-frā´-zhə] abnormally rapid yet fluent and articulate speech |
| **sphygm** | Greek — pulse<br>**sphygmic** [sfĭg´-mĭk] of or pertaining to the circulatory pulse | **tachisto** | Greek — fast<br>**tachistoscope** [tă-kĭs´-tə-skōp] instrument for rapidly showing images on a screen to test perception |
| **sphygmo** | Greek — pulse<br>**sphygmomanometer** [sfĭg-mō-mə-nŏm´-ə-tər] an instrument which measures blood pressure in the arteries | **ten** | Latin — hold<br>**detention** [dĭ-tĕn´-shən] the act of detaining or holding back<br>**retentive** [rĭ-tĕn´-tĭv] tending to retain or hold on to<br>**tenable** [tĕn´-ə-bəl] able to be held for a specified time<br>**tenacious** [tĕ-nā´-shəs] holding firmly<br>**tenure** [tĕn´-yər] the term during which some position is held<br>**untenable** [ən-tĕn´-ə-bəl] not able to be defended or justified |
| **sphyx** | Greek — pulse<br>**asphyxiation** [ăs-fĭk-sē-ā´-shən] act or process of causing suffocation | | |
| **stas** | Greek — standing still<br>**ecstasy** [ĕk´-stə-sē] a state beyond reason and self-control; overwhelming emotion | | |
| **stat** | Greek — standing still<br>**stationary** [stā´-shə-nĕr-ē] fixed in position | **terr** | Latin — earth<br>**mediterranean** [mĕd-ĭ-tə-rā´-nē-ən] enclosed or nearly enclosed with land |
| **statis** | Greek — standing still<br>**statistics** [stə-tĭs´-tĭks] a collection of numerical data, facts | **therap** | Greek — treatment<br>**cryotherapy** [krī-ō-thĕr´-ə-pē] therapeutic use of cold<br>**hypnotherapy** [hĭp-nō-thĕr´-ə-pē] the use of hypnosis in treating illness or emotional problems<br>**phytotherapy** [fī-tō-thĕr´-ə-pē] the use of herbs and other plants to promote health and treat disease<br>**pyretotherapy** [pīr-ĭ-tō-thĕr´-ə-pē] fever therapy |
| **surg** | Latin — rise<br>**insurgent** [ĭn-sür´-jənt] person involved in a rebellion against a constituted authority<br>**resurgence** [rē´-sür-jənts] arising again into life, activity, or prominence | | |
| **surrect** | Latin — rise<br>**insurrection** [ĭn-sə-rĕk´-shən] a rising up against established authority | **therm** | Greek — heat<br>**xerothermic** [zir-ə-thûr´-mĭk] of or pertaining to a hot and dry climactic period |
| **tach** | Greek — fast<br>**tachycardia** [tăk-ĭ-kär´-dē-ə] an abnormally fast heartbeat<br>**tachygraphy** [tă-kĭg´-rə-fē] the art or technique of rapid writing or shorthand<br>**tachymeter** [tă´-kŏm´-ĭ-tər] device for measuring speed of rotation | **thes** | Greek — to place, to put<br>**antithesis** [ăn-tĭth´-ĭ-sĭs] exact opposite, contrast |

**narcosynthesis** [när-kō-sĭn´-thə-sĭs] a treatment of neurosis, requiring a patient to be under the influence of a hypnotic drug

**synthesize** [sĭn´-thə-sīz] combine so as to form a more complex product, etc.

**thesis** [thē´-sĭs] the central idea in a piece of writing

**thet**  Greek — to place, to put
**antithetic** [ăn-tə-thĕt´-ĭk] directly contrasting or opposite

**thorax**  Greek — chest
**cephalothorax** [sĕf-ĕ-lō-thôr´-ăks] fused head and thorax of an arachnid or higher crustacean

**tme**  Greek — cut
**tmesis** [tə-mē´-sĭs] separation of a compound word by interposition of another word

**tom**  Greek — cut
**atomize** [ăt´-ə-mīz] to reduce to minute particles

**tome**  Greek — cut
**epitome** [ĭ-pĭt´-ə-mē] a summary or typical example of something
**microtome** [mī´-krə-tōm] scientific instrument that cuts thin slices of biological tissues for microscopic examination

**tomy**  Greek — cut
**anatomy** [ə-năt´-tə-mē] the scientific study of the body and how its parts are arranged
**appendectomy** [ăp-ən-dĕk´-tə-mē] the surgical removal of the appendix
**esophagotomy** [ĭ-săf-ə-gŏt´-ə-mē] incision through the wall of the esophagus (Medical)

**traumat**  Greek — shock or wound
**post-traumatic** [pōst-trə-măt´-ĭk] occurring as a result of or after injury
**traumatic** [trə-măt´-ĭk] relating to a physical or emotional wound

**traumatize** [trô´-mə-tīz] experience severe emotional distress

**trop**  Greek — turn
**anemotropism** [ăn-ə-mŏ-trə´-pĭz-əm] orientation in response to air currents

**troph**  Greek — nourish
**atrophy** [ă´-trə-fē] to waste away or to decrease in size as of a body part or tissue
**dystrophy** [dĭs´-trə-fē] any degenerative disorder resulting from inadequate or faulty nutrition
**hypertrophy** [hī-pûr´-trə-fē] excessive growth or enlargement of a body part or organ
**trophic** [trō´-fĭk] of or relating to nutrition

**trude**  Latin — thrust
**intrude** [ĭn-trood´] to enter uninvited
**protrude** [prō-trood´] to bulge or extend forward

**trus**  Latin — thrust
**extrusion** [ĕk-stroo´-zhən] the action of squeezing something out by pressure
**intrusion** [ĭn-troo´-zhən] a disturbance; an invasion of someone's privacy
**protrusive** [prō-troo´-sĭv] jutting or thrusting forward
**unobtrusive** [ŭn-əb-troo´-sĭv] inconspicuous; not standing out

**tum**  Latin — swell
**contumacious** [kän-tü-mā´-shəs] willfully obstinate
**tumescence** [too-mĕs´-əns] condition of being swollen or enlarged
**tumultuous** [tə-mul´-choo-əs] full of commotion and uproar

**tumori**  Latin — swell
**tumorigenic** [too-mər-ĭ-jĭn´-ĭk] producing or tending to produce tumors

| | |
|---|---|
| **turb** | Latin — commotion, agitation<br>**disturbance** [dĭ-stûr´-bəns] an interruption of a state of peace or quiet<br>**perturb** [pər-tûrb´] to disturb greatly; to upset<br>**turbidity** [tûr-bĭd´-ĭ-tē] muddiness created by stirring up sediment or by having foreign particles suspended<br>**turbine** [tûr´-bīn] a machine for producing power in which a wheel is made to revolve by a fast-moving flow of water, steam, gas, or air<br>**turbulence** [tûr´-byə-ləns] a state of confusion and disorder |
| **type** | Greek — model, impression<br>**archetype** [är´-kĭ-tīp] an original model on which something is patterned; prototype |
| **typh** | Greek — stupor, fog<br>**pyretotyphosis**<br>[pĭ-rə-tō-tĭ´-fō-sĭs] the delirium of fever |
| **urg** | Greek — work, power<br>**metallurgy** [mĕt´-l-ûr-jē] the science and technology of extracting metals from their ores<br>**pyrometallurgy**<br>[pī-rō-mĕt´-l-ûr-jē] chemical metallurgy that depends on heat action |
| **verm** | Latin — worm<br>**vermin** [vûr´-mĕn] any of various small animals or insects that are pests; e.g.; cockroaches or rats<br>**verminous** [vûr´-mə-nəs] of the nature of vermin; very offensive or repulsive |
| **vermi** | Latin — worm<br>**vermicelli** [vûr-mə-chĕl´-ē] pasta in strings thinner than spaghetti<br>**vermicide** [vûr´-mə-sīd] a substance used to kill worms<br>**vermifugal** [vûr-mə-fyo͞o´-gəl] tending to expel worms |

| | |
|---|---|
| | **vermiphobia** [vûr-mə-fō´-bē-ə] fear of worms<br>**vermivorous** [vûr-mĭv´-ər-əs] feeding on worms |
| **visc** | Latin — sticky<br>**viscidly** [vĭs´-ĭd-lē] in a sticky manner<br>**viscosity** [vĭs-kŏs´-sĭ-tē] thickness of a liquid or its resistance to flow<br>**viscous** [vĭs´-kəs] thick and sticky; not free-flowing |
| **visco** | Latin — sticky<br>**viscoelasticity**<br>[vĭs-kō-ĭ-lăs-tĭ´-sĭ-tē] being both viscous and elastic simultaneously<br>**viscometer** [vĭ-skŏm´-ĭ-tər] instrument for measuring viscosity |
| **vor** | Latin — eat<br>**vermivorous** [vûr-mĭv´-ər-əs] feeding on worms |
| **xer** | Greek — dry<br>**xerophthalmia** [zĭr-əf-thăl´-mē-ə] excessive dryness of the conjunctiva and cornea of the eye (Medical) |
| **xero** | [combining form] Greek — dry<br>**xeroderma** [zĭr-ô-dûr´-mə] abnormal dryness of the skin (Medical)<br>**xerographic** [zĭr-ə-grăf´-ĕk] related to electrophotography or dry photocopying<br>**xerography** [zĭ-rŏg´-rə-fē] method of dry photocopying in which the image is transferred by using the forces of electric charges<br>**xerophagy** [zĭ-rof´-ə-jē] eating of dry food<br>**xerophyte** [zĭr´-ə-fīt] a plant structurally adapted for growth in dry conditions<br>**xerothermic** [zĭr-ə-thûr´-mĭk] of or pertaining to a hot and dry climactic period |
| **xyl** | Greek — wood<br>**xyloid** [zī´-loid] resembling or like wood in nature |

**xylose** [zī´-lōz] a sugar extracted from wood

**xylo**   [combining form] Greek — wood

**xylographer** [zī-lŏg´-rə-fər] one who is skilled in artistic wood carving

**xylology** [zī-lŏ´-lō-gē] the study of the structure of wood

**xylophagous** [zī-lŏf´-ə-gəs] feeding on wood

**xylophone** [zī´-lə-fōn] a musical instrument of flat, wooden bars of different lengths that produce notes when hit with sticks

**zygo**   Greek — paired

**zygodactyl** [zī-gō-dăk´-təl] having the toes arranged two in front and two behind

# GREEK AND LATIN SUFFIXES

**-able** Latin — able to be
**comfortable** [kəm′-fərt-ə-bəl] more than adequate
**culpable** [kŭl′-pə-bəl] deserving blame
**implacable** [ĭm-plă′-kə-bəl] not capable of being appeased or pacified
**tenable** [tĕn′-ə-bəl] able to be held for a specified time
**untenable** [ən-tĕn′-ə-bəl] not able to be defended or justified

**i-ac** Greek — one who; related to, pertaining to
**insomniac** [ĭn-sŏm′-nē-ăk] person who is unable to sleep

**-acious** Latin — having the quality of
**contumacious** [kän-tü-mā′-shəs] willfully obstinate
**tenacious** [tĕ-nā′-shəs] holding firmly

**-age** Latin — state, quality, act
**appendage** [ə-pĕn′-dĭj] a projecting body part; a secondary attachment
**collage** [kə-läzh′] an artistic composition made of various materials, such as paper, cloth, or wood, glued on a surface
**foliage** [fō′-lē-ĭj] leaves, as of a plant or tree

**-al** Latin — like, related to; an action or process
**branchial** [brăng′-kē-əl] of or relating to gills
**medieval** [mēd-ē′-vəl] relating or belonging to the Middle Ages
**patriarchal** [pā-trē-är′kəl] relating to or characteristic of a culture ruled by men
**vermifugal** [vûr-mə-fyo͞o′-gəl] tending to expel worms

**i-al** Latin — like, related to; an action or process
**exponential** [ĕk-spō-nĕn′-shəl] characterized by an extremely rapid increase

**fluvioglacial** [flo͞o-vē-ō-glā′-shəl] pertaining to streams flowing from glaciers or to the deposits made by such streams (Geology)
**influential** [ĭn-flo͞o-ən′-shəl] having a great deal of power to change something
**sequential** [sē-kwĕn′-shəl] following in regular succession without gaps

**ic-al** Latin — like, related to; an action or process
**physical** [fĭz′-ĭ-kəl] of or relating to the body
**physically** [fĭz′-ĭ-kəl-lē] in a physical manner; in respect to the body

**n-al** Latin — like, related to; an action or process
**paternal** [pə-tûr′-nəl] related on the father's side

**ygi-al** Latin — like, related to; an action or process
**apterygial** [ăp-tə-rĭj′-ē-əl] belonging to the group of animals without paired wings, fins, or limbs

**-an** Latin — like, related to
**median** [mē′-dē-ən] related to or situated in the middle

**-ance** Latin — state, quality, act
**disturbance** [dĭ-stûr′-bəns] an interruption of a state of peace or quiet

**-anean** Latin — having the quality of
**mediterranean** [mĕd-ĭ-tə-rā′-nē-ən] enclosed or nearly enclosed with land

**-ant** Latin — one who, that which; state, quality
**desiccant** [dĕs′-ə-kənt] a substance that promotes drying
**pendant** [pĕn′-dənt] an ornamental, hanging object

**id-ant**   Latin — one who, that which; state, quality
**antioxidant** [ăn-tī-ŏk´-sə-dənt] substance that counteracts oxidation

**-arious**   Latin — of, related to
**gregarious** [grĭ-găr´-ē-əs] fond of company; sociable

**-arium**   Latin — place where
**glaciarium** [glā-shē-ăr´-ē-ŭm] a skating rink with a floor of artificial ice

**-ary**   Latin — that which; someone or something that belongs to; of, related to; one who
**cinerary** [sĕn´-ə-ră-rē] containing or used for ashes
**glossary** [glôs´-ə-rē] an alphabetical list of specialized words with their definitions, usually at the back of a book
**intermediary** [ĭn-tər-mē´-dē-ĕr-ē] a negotiator who acts as a link between parties
**stationary** [stā´-shə-nĕr-ē] fixed in position

**-ate**   Latin — to make, to act; one who, that which
**abranchiate** [ā-brăng´-kē-ĭt] lacking gills
**coarctate** [cō-ärk´-tāt] pressed together; closely connected
**desiccate** [des´-ə-kāt] to dry completely; to deprive of moisture
**exculpate** [ĕks-kŭl´-pāt] to clear from alleged fault or guilt; to free from blame
**exfoliate** [ĕks-fō´-lē-āt] flake or peel of
**expatriate** [ĕks-pā´-trē-āt] someone who no longer lives in his or her own country
**expurgate** [ĕks´-pər-gāt] to edit, to censor
**inculpate** [ĭn-kŭl´-pāt] to incriminate; to blame
**intermediate** [ĭn-tər-mē´-dē-ĭt] being or happening between two other related things, levels, or points

**magnate** [măg´-nāt] a person of high rank, power, influence, etc. in a specific field
**placate** [plā´-kāt] to soothe or mollify; appease
**segregate** [sĕg´-rĭ-gāt] to set apart from the rest or from each other

**-ation**   Latin — an action or process
**coarctation** [cō-ärk-tā´-shən] a narrowing or constriction
**congregation** [kŏn-grĭ-gā´-shən] a group of people or things gathered together; gathering
**desiccation** [dĕs-ə-kā´-shən] the process of extracting moisture
**exasperation** [ĭg-zăs-pə-rā´-shən] annoyance and frustration
**incantation** [ĭn-kăn-tā´-shən] the chanting of supposedly magic words
**mediation** [mē-dē-ā´-shən] the process of resolving differences
**oxygenation** [ŏk-sē-jĕ-nā´-shən] the process of providing oxygen
**repatriation** [rē-pă-trē´-ā-shən] the act of returning to one's country of origin

**ific-ation**   Latin — an action or process
**fortification** [fōrt-ə-fə-kā´-shən] the act or process of strengthening
**mollification** [mŏl-ə-fĭ-kā´-shən] appeasement

**i-ation**   Latin — an action or process
**asphyxiation** [ăs-fĭk-sē-ā´-shən] act or process of causing suffocation
**deglaciation** [dē-glā-sē-ā´-shən] the gradual melting away of a glacier from the surface of a landmass
**glaciation** [glā-sē-ā´-shən] the process of being covered or covering with masses of ice

**fic-ation**   Latin — an action or process
**magnification** [măg-nĭ-fĭ-kā´-shən] the process of making something look bigger than it really is

**ill-ation**   Latin — an action or process
**cantillation** [kăn-tə-lā´-shən] the action of unaccompanied chanting in free rhythm

**it-ation** Latin — an action or process
**felicitation** [fĭ-lĭs-ĭ-tā´-shən] an expression of pleasure at the success or good fortune of another

**iz-ation** Latin — an action or process
**cinematization** [sĭn-ə-mə-tĭ-zā´-shən] the process of adapting a novel, play, etc. for film or movies

**tu-ation** Latin — an action or process
**fluctuation** [flŭk-chōō-ā´-shən] variation in level, degree; constant change

**-cene** Greek — new, recent
**Eocene** [ē´-ə-sēn] relating to the second epoch of the Tertiary period

**-celli** Latin — small
**vermicelli** [vûr-mə-chĕl´-ē] pasta in strings thinner than spaghetti

**-cide** Latin — kill
**patricide** [păt´-rə-sīd] the killing of a father by his own child
**vermicide** [vûr´-mə-sīd] a substance used to kill worms

**usca-cide** Latin — kill
**molluscacide** [mə-lə´-skə-sīd] a chemical pesticide used to kill mollusks

**i-cle** Latin — small
**canticle** [kăn´-tĭ-kəl] a hymn derived from the Bible; literally, a "little" song

**-ebo** Latin — something tending to
**placebo** [plə-sē´-bō] something done or said simply to reassure

**-ence** Latin — state, quality, act
**affluence** [ăf´-lōō-ăns] an abundance of material wealth
**consequence** [kŏn´-sə-kwĕns] the effect, result, or outcome of something occurring earlier
**magniloquence** [măg-nĭl´-ə-kwəns] excessive use of verbal ornamentation; pompous discourse
**resurgence** [rē-sûr´-jəns] a rising again into life, activity, or prominence

**-ency** Latin — state, quality, act
**fluency** [flōō´-ən-sē] effortless expression

**fic-ence** Latin — state, quality, act
**magnificence** [măg-nĭ´-fĭ-səns] splendid or grand in size or appearance

**ul-ence** Latin — state, quality, act
**turbulence** [tûr´-byə-ləns] a state of confusion and disorder

**-ent** Latin — one who, that which; like, related to
**complacent** [kəm-plā´-sənt] overly pleased with oneself or one's situation; smug
**component** [kəm-pō´-nənt] a part of something larger
**effluent** [ĕf´-lōō-ənt] flowing outward or forward
**exponential** [ĕk-spō-nĕn´-shəl] characterized by an extremely rapid increase
**influential** [ĭn-flōō-ən´-shəl] having a great deal of power to change something
**insurgent** [ĭn-sûr´-jənt] person involved in a rebellion against a constituted authority
**opponent** [ə-pō´-nənt] one who takes an opposite position; rival
**proponent** [prō-pō´-nənt] one who argues in favor of something; advocate
**sequential** [sē-kwĕn´-shəl] following in regular succession without gaps
**subsequent** [sŭb´-sə-kwənt] happening or existing after; later

**i-ent** Latin - one who, that which; like, related to
**emollient** [ə-mŏl´-yənt] something that has a softening or soothing effect

**-er** Latin — one who, that which
**anther** [ăn´-thər] the part of a flower that contains pollen
**selenographer** [sĕl-lə-nŏg´-rə-fûr] expert in mapping the physical features of the moon
**xylographer** [zī-lŏg´-rə-fər] one who is skilled in artistic wood carving

**-escence** Latin — growing
**tumescence** [too-měs´-əns] condition of being swollen or enlarged

**-escent** Latin — becoming, having
**mollescent** [mə-lě´-sənt] softening or tending to soften

**-esia** Greek — action, process
**anesthekinesia** [ăn-ĭs-thē-kĭ-nē´-zhə] loss of sensibility and motor power
**anesthesia** [ăn-ĭs-thē´-zhə] medically induced insensitivity to pain

**-esis** Greek — action
**kinesthesis** [kĭn-ĭs-thē´-sĕs] the ability to feel movements of the limbs and body

**-ete** Old French — one who
**aesthete** [ěs´-thēt] one who has or affects artistic perception or appreciation of beauty

**l-eum** Latin — that which
**petroleum** [pə-trō´-lē-əm] crude oil that occurs naturally in sedimentary rocks and consists mainly of hydrocarbons

**i-ferous** Latin — producing
**somniferous** [sŏm-nĭf´-ər-əs] sleep inducing

**li-ferous** Latin — producing
**petroliferous** [pě-trə-lĭf´-ər-əs] containing or yielding petroleum

**-fy** Latin — to do, to make, to act
**magnify** [măg´-nĭ-fī] to increase in size; enlarge

**i-fy** Latin — to do, to make, to act
**fortify** [fôr´-tə-fī] to strengthen, especially in order to protect
**mollify** [mŏl´-ə-fī] to soothe the temper of; appease; soften
**petrify** [pět´-trə-fī] to turn organic matter into stone

**-ia** Greek — condition
**agoraphobia** [ăg-ə-rə-fō´-bē-ə] an abnormal fear of being in open or public places

**amnesia** [ăm-nē´-zhə] loss of the ability to remember
**aortarctia** [ā-ôr-tark´-shə] narrowing of the aorta
**cryptomnesia** [krĭp-təm-nē´-zhə] a condition whereby experiences are believed to be original, but are actually based on memories of forgotten events
**dyspepsia** [dĭs-pěp´-sē-ə] indigestion
**echolalia** [ěk-ō-lā´-lē-ə] involuntary parrot-like repetition of a word or phrase just spoken by another; echoing
**ergophobia** [ər-gə-fō´-bē-ə] abnormal and persistent fear of work or the workplace
**eupepsia** [yoo-pěp´-sē-ə] good digestion
**euphoria** [yoo-fōr´-ē-ə] feeling of great joy, excitement, or well-being, almost to the point of exaggeration
**glossolalia** [glŏs-ō-lā´-lē-ə] repetitive non-meaningful speech
**hypnophobia** [hĭp-nə-fō´-bē-ə] an abnormal fear of falling asleep
**narcohypnia** [när-kō-hĭp´-nē-ə] numbness experienced upon awakening
**tachycardia** [tăk-ĭ-kär´-dē-ə] an abnormally fast heartbeat
**tachyphrasia** [tăk-ĭ-frā´-zhə] abnormally rapid yet fluent and articulate speech
**vermiphobia** [vûr-mə-fō´-bē-ə] fear of worms
**xerophthalmia** [zĭr-əf-thăl´-mē-ə] excessive dryness of the conjunctiva and cornea of the eye (Medical)

**ic-ian** Latin — one who
**physician** [fĭ-zĭsh´-ən] a person skilled in the art of healing

**t-ible** Latin — able to be
**combustible** [kəm-bŭs´-tə-bəl] able to burn easily
**incombustible** [ĭn-kəm-bŭs´-tə-bəl] not capable of being burned

**-ic** Latin — like, related to
**anechoic** [ăn-ě-kō´-ĭk] free from echoes and reverberations

**antipyretic** [ăn-tē-pĭ-rĕt´-ĭk] drug that relieves or reduces fever

**antithetic** [ăn-tə-thĕt´-ĭk] directly contrasting or opposite

**apyretic** [ā-pī-rĕt´-ĭk] without fever

**archaic** [är-kā´-ĭk] belonging to an earlier period; ancient

**barometric** [băr-ə-mĕ´-trĭk] related to or indicated by a barometer

**cephalic** [sĕ-făl´-ĭk] of, or relating to, the head

**cinematic** [sĭn-ə-măt´-ĭk] relating to the production or showing of motion pictures

**cryophilic** [krī-ō-fĭl´-ĭk] capable of living at low temperatures

**dimorphic** [dī-môr´-fĭk] occurring or existing in two different forms

**echoic** [ĕ-kō´-ĭk] formed in imitation of some natural sound

**ergogenic** [ûr-gə-jĕn´-ĭk] increasing capacity for physical or mental labor

**isobaric** [ī-sə-bär´-ĭk] showing equal pressure

**orthoscopic** [ôr-thō-skŏp´-ĭk] related to seeing an image in correct and normal proportion

**Paleolithic** [pā-lē-ə-lĭth´-ĭk] related to the early Stone Age

**peptic** [pĕp´-tĭk] relating to digestion

**petrographic** [pĕt-rə-grăf´-ĭk] related to the systematic description and classification of rocks using microscopic examination

**phytomorphic** [fī-tō-môr´-fĭk] having attributes of a plant

**post-traumatic** [pōst-trə-măt´-ĭk] occurring as a result of or after injury

**pyrogenic** [pī-rō-jĕn´-ĭk] fever inducing

**selenocentric** [sə-lē-nə-sĕn´-trĭk] of or relating to the center of the moon; having the moon as center

**sphygmic** [sfĭg´-mĭk] of or pertaining to the circulatory pulse

**traumatic** [trə-măt´-ĭk] relating to a physical or emotional wound

**trophic** [trō´-fĭk] of or relating to nutrition

**tumorigenic** [tōō-mər-ĭ-jĭn´-ĭk] producing or tending to produce tumors

**xerographic** [zir-ə-grăf´-ĭk] related to electrophotography or dry photocopying

**xerothermic** [zir-ə-thûr´-mĭk] of or pertaining to a hot and dry climactic period

**et-ic** Latin — like, related to

**aesthetic** [ĕs-thĕt´-ĭk] relating to the enjoyment or study of beauty

**anesthetic** [ăn-ĭs-thĕt´-ĭk] a drug that causes temporary loss of bodily sensations

**kinetic** [kə-nĕ´-tĭk] related to movement

**ist-ic** Latin — like, related to

**antagonistic** [ăn-tăg-ə-nĭst´-ĭk] contending with or opposing another; adversarial

**holistic** [hō-lĭs´-tĭk] involving all of something

**on-ic** Latin — like, related to

**mnemonic** [nĭ-mŏn´-ĭk] a short rhyme, phrase, etc. for making information easier to remember

**st-ic** Latin — like, related to

**acoustic** [ə-kōō´-stĭk] related to hearing or to sound as it is heard

**t-ic** Latin — like, related to

**hypnotic** [hĭp-nŏt´-ĭk] relating to or involving sleep or hypnosis

**narcotic** [när-kŏ´-tĭk] a drug used to relieve pain and induce sleep

**-ics** Latin — science, related to, system

**cryogenics** [krī-ō-jĕn´-ĭks] the science that deals with the production of extremely low temperatures (Physics)

**ergonomics** [ûr-gə-nôm´-ĭks] the scientific design of products, machines, etc. to maximize user safety, comfort, and efficiency

**hieroglyphics** [hī-rə-glĭf´-ĭks] the picture script of the ancient Egyptian priesthood

**metaphysics** [mĕt-ə-fĭz´-ĭks] a branch of philosophy dealing with the nature of reality

**orthodontics** [ôr-thə-dŏn′-tĭks] the branch of dentistry concerned with the prevention or correction of irregularities of the teeth
**physics** [fĭz′-ĭks] related to matter and energy and their interactions

**t-ics**    Latin — science, related to, system
**orthotics** [ôr-thə′-tĭks] the science that deals with the developing and fitting of medical devices
**statistics** [stə-tĭs′-tĭks] a collection of numerical data, facts

**-id**    Latin — like, related to
**placid** [plăs′-ĕd] calm in nature; tranquil
**placidity** [plə-sĭd′-ĭ-tē] the quality or feeling of being calm or composed

**-ide**    Latin — thing belonging to
**dioxide** [dī-ŏk′-sīd] an oxide containing two atoms of oxygen in the molecule
**peptide** [pĕp′-tīd] a compound with amino bonds
**peroxide** [pə-rŏk′-sīd] an oxide containing a relatively high proportion of oxygen

**-ier**    Latin — that which
**glacier** [glā′-shər] a slowly moving mass of ice

**-in**    Latin — like, related to; thing which
**melanin** [mĕl′-ə-nĭn] a brownish-black pigment found in skin
**vermin** [vûr′-mĭn] any of various small animals or insects that are pests; e.g. cockroaches or rats
**verminous** [vûr′-mə-nəs] of the nature of vermin; very offensive or repulsive

**-ine**    Latin — like, related to
**turbine** [tûr′-bīn] a machine for producing power in which a wheel is made to revolve by a fast-moving flow of water, steam, gas, or air

**all-ine**    Latin — like, related to
**crystalline** [krĭs′-tə-lĭn] of the nature of crystals

**-ing**    Old English — related to
**impending** [ĭm-pĕn′-dĭng] that is about to occur; imminent

**-ion**    Latin — an action or process; state, quality, act
**concussion** [kən-kŭsh′-ən] an injury to the brain, often resulting from a blow to the head
**deglaciation** [dē-glā-sē-ā′-shən] the gradual melting away of a glacier from the surface of a landmass
**echolocation** [ĕk-ō-lō-kā′-shən] a means of locating an object using an emitted sound and the reflection back from it
**exasperation** [ĭg-zăs-pə-rā′-shən] annoyance and frustration
**extrusion** [ĕk-strōō′-zhən] the action of squeezing something out by pressure
**glaciation** [glā-sē-ā′-shən] the process of being covered or covering with masses of ice
**insurrection** [ĭn-sə-rĕk′-shən] a rising up against established authority
**intrusion** [ĕn-trōō′-zhən] a disturbance; an invasion of someone's privacy
**percussion** [pər-kŭsh′-ən] the group of instruments that produces sound by being struck, such as drums, cymbals, and tambourines
**stationary** [stā′-shə-nĕr-ē] fixed in position
**suspension** [sə-spĕn′-shən] an interruption; literally, "to be left hanging"

**-ions**    Latin — an action or process; state, quality, act
**repercussions** [rē-pər-kŭsh′-əns] the effects, often indirect or remote, of some event or action

**-is**    Latin — thing which
**antithesis** [ăn-tĭth′-ĭ-sĭs] exact opposite, contrast
**epiglottis** [ĕp-ə-glŏt′-əs] a small flap at the back of the tongue that covers the windpipe during swallowing
**narcosynthesis** [när-kō-sĭn′-thə-sĭs] a treatment of neurosis, requiring a patient to be under the influence of a hypnotic drug

**thesis** [thē′-sĭs] the central idea in a piece of writing

**-ism**    Latin — act, state, condition
**anemotropism** [ăn-ə-mŏ-trə′-pĭz-əm] orientation in response to air currents

**-ist**    Latin — one who
**anesthesiologist**
[ăn-ĭs-thē-zē-ä′-lə-jĭst] a doctor who specializes in administering drugs to prevent or relieve pain during surgery
**glaciologist** [glā-sē-ŏl′-ə-jĭst] an expert in the formation, movements, etc. of glaciers
**orthopedist** [ôr-thə-pēd′-ĭst] a specialist in correcting deformities of the skeletal system especially in children
**protagonist** [prō-tăg-ə-nĕst′] key figure in a contest or dispute; main character in a novel
**somnambulist** [sŏm-năm′-byə-lĭst] sleepwalker

**ic-ist**    Latin — one who
**physicist** [fĭz′-ə-sĭst] a scientist whose specialty is physics

**t-ist**    Latin — one who
**hypnotist** [hĭp′-nə-tĭst] a person who uses hypnosis as a form of treatment

**-itis**    Greek — inflammation
**encephalitis** [ĕn-sĕf-ə-lī′-tĭs] inflammation of the brain
**glossitis** [glô-sī′-təs] inflammation of the tongue

**-ity**    Latin — state, quality, act
**asperity** [ă-spĕr′-ĭ-tē] harshness or severity of manner or tone
**felicity** [fĭ-lĭs′-ə-tē] pleasing and appropriate manner; happiness
**purity** [pyo͞or′-ĭ-tē] the quality or state of being clean

**ic-ity**    Latin — state, quality, act
**viscoelasticity**
[vĭs-kō-ĭ-lăs-tĭ′-sĭ-tē] being both viscous and elastic simultaneously

**id-ity**    Latin — state, quality, act
**placidity** [plə-sĭd′-ĭ-tē] the quality or feeling of being calm or composed
**turbidity** [tûr-bĭd′-ĭ-tē] muddiness created by stirring up sediment or by having foreign particles suspended

**n-ity**    Latin — state, quality, act
**paternity** [pə-tûr′-nə-tē] the fact or state of being a father; fatherhood

**s-ity**    Latin — state, quality, act
**viscosity** [vĭs-kŏs′-sĭ-tē] thickness of a liquid or its resistance to flow

**-ium**    Latin — chemical element
**selenium** [sə-lə′-nē-əm] a trace mineral that has light-sensitive properties

**-ive**    Latin — tending to or performing
**pensive** [pĕn′-sĭv] thoughtfully weighing an issue or problem
**protrusive** [prō-tro͞o′-sĭv] jutting or thrusting forward
**unobtrusive** [ŭn-əb-tro͞o′-sĭv] inconspicuous; not standing out

**at-ive**    Latin — tending to or performing
**siccative** [sĭk′-ə-tĭv] causing to dry; drying

**t-ive**    Latin — tending to or performing
**retentive** [rĭ-tĕn′-tĭv] tending to retain or hold on to

**-ize**    Latin — to make, to act
**atomize** [ăt′-ə-mīz] to reduce to minute particles
**energize** [ĕn′-ər-jīz] to make active
**synthesize** [sĭn′-thə-sīz] combine so as to form a more complex product, etc.
**traumatize** [trô′-mə-tīz] experience severe emotional distress

**all-ize**    Latin — to make, to act
**crystallize** [krĭs′-tə-līz] cause to form crystals

**-lite**    Greek — stone
**ichthyolite** [ĭk-thē′-ō-līt] a fossil fish or fragment of a fish

**-logy**   Greek — study of, science

**anemology** [ăn-ə-mŏl´-ə-jē] the study of the movements of the winds

**dactylology** [dăk-těl-lĭ´-lä-jē] the science of communicating by using hand signs; sign language

**ichthyology** [ĭk-thē-ŏl´-ə-jē] the study of fishes

**petrology** [pə-trŏl´-ə-jē] the study of the origin, formation, and composition of rocks

**phytology** [fī-tŏl´-ə-jē] the study of plants; botany

**selenology** [sě-lə-nŏl´-ə-jē] the study of the origin and physical characteristics of the moon

**xylology** [zī-lŏ´-lō-gē] the study of the structure of wood

**ical-ly**   Old English — in the manner of

**physically** [fĭz´-ĭ-kə-lē] in a physical manner; in respect to the body

**id-ly**   Old English — in the manner of

**viscidly** [vĭs´-ĭd-lē] in a sticky manner

**-ma**   Latin — something done

**dogma** [dôg´-mə] something held as an established opinion

**-ment**   Latin — that which

**postponement** [pōst-pōn´-mənt] the act of putting something off to a future time

**-mony**   Latin — state, quality, that which

**patrimony** [păt´-rə-mō-nē] an estate inherited from one's father or ancestor

**-oid**   Greek — resembling

**colloid** [kăl´-oid] a gelatinous substance

**xyloid** [zī´-loid] resembling or like wood in nature

**yg-oid**   Greek — resembling

**pterygoid** [těr´-ə-goid] like a bird's wing in form or limbs

**-olog**   Greek — study of, science

**anesthesiologist** [ăn-ĭs-thē-zē-ä´-lə-jĭst] a doctor who specializes in administering drugs to prevent or relieve pain during surgery

**i-olog**   Greek — study of, science

**glaciologist** [glā-sē-ŏl´-ə-jĭst] an expert in the formation, movements, etc. of glaciers

**-ology**   Greek — study of, science

**doxology** [dŏk-sŏl´-ə-jē] a liturgical formula of praise to God

**morphology** [môr-fŏl´-ə-jē] the study of the form and structure of organisms

**esi-ology**   Greek — study of, science

**kinesiology** [kə-nē-sē-ŏl´-ə-jē] the study of human musculoskeletal movement

**i-ology**   Greek — study of, science

**glaciology** [glā-sē-ŏl´-ə-jē] the scientific study of the nature, formation, and movement of glaciers

**physiology** [fĭz-ē-ŏl´-ə-jē] the branch of the biological sciences that deals with the functioning of organisms

**id-ology**   Greek — study of, science

**pteridology** [těr-ĭ-dŏl´-ə-jē] the branch of botany that studies ferns

**-oma**   Greek — growth, tumor

**melenoma** [měl-ə-nō´-mə] a type of skin cancer that appears as a dark mark or growth on the skin

**-on**   Greek — quality, state

**oxymoron** [ŏk-sē-môr´-ŏn] a combination of contradictory or incongruous words

**tachyon** [tăk´-ē-ŏn] a hypothetical subatomic particle that can travel faster than the speed of light

**at-or**   Latin — one who, that which; condition, state, quality

**incinerator** [ĭn-sĭn´-ə-rā-tər] a furnace for burning waste under controlled conditions

**at-ory**   Latin — place where

**lavatory** [lăv´-ə-tôr-ē] a room equipped with toilet facilities

**-ose**   Latin — having the quality of, a carbohydrate

**foliose** [fō´-lē-ōs] covered with leaves; leafy

**xylose** [zī´-lōz] a sugar extracted from wood

**-osis**   Greek — condition

**hypnosis** [hĭp-nō´-sĭs] a state that resembles sleep but is induced by suggestion

**ichthyosis** [ĭk-thē-ō´-sĭs] congenital disease in which the skin is fishlike (dry and scaly)(Medical)

**metamorphosis** [mĕt-ə-môr´-fə-sĭs] a complete change of character, appearance, condition, etc.

**narcosis** [när-kō´-sĭs] a state of stupor or greatly reduced activity produced by a drug or other element

**pyretotyphosis** [pī-rə-tō-tī´fō-sĭs] the delirium of fever

**selenosis** [sĕ-lə-nō´-sĭs] poisoning caused by ingesting dangerously high amounts of selenium

**-ous**   Latin — having the quality of

**amorphous** [ə-môr´-fəs] without definite form; shapeless

**anemophilous** [ăn-ə-mŏf´-ə-ləs] pollinated by the wind

**anthophagous** [ăn-thŏ´-fə-gəs] feeding on flowers

**anthropophagous** [än-thrə-pŏf´-ə-gəs] feeding on human flesh; cannibalistic

**brachypterous** [bră-kĭp´-tər-əs] short winged

**collagenous** [kə-lä´-jə-nəs] forming or producing collagen

**ichthyophagous** [ĭk-thē-ä´-fə-gəs] fish-eating

**magnanimous** [măg-năn´-ə-məs] generous, noble, and understanding in spirit

**phyllophagous** [fĭ-lŏf´-ə-gəs] feeding on leaves; leaf-eating

**phytophagous** [fĭ-tŏf´-ə-gəs] plant-eating; herbivorous

**verminous** [vûr´-mə-nəs] of the nature of vermin; very offensive or repulsive

**vermivorous** [vûr-mĭv´-ər-əs] feeding on worms

**viscous** [vĭs´-kəs] thick and sticky; not free-flowing

**xylophagous** [zī-lŏf´-ə-gəs] feeding on wood

**i-ous**   Latin — having the quality of

**obsequious** [ŏb-sē´-kwē-əs] overly eager to please or obey

**it-ous**   Latin — having the quality of

**infelicitous** [ĭn-fə-lĭs´-ĭ-təs] unsuitable; inappropriate

**-sis**   Greek — action, process

**tmesis** [tə-mē´-sĭs] separation of a compound word by interposition of another word

**-tion**   Latin — state, condition, act

**ablution** [ă-blōō´-shən] a washing of the body, especially as a religious ceremony

**combustion** [kəm-bŭs´-chən] act or process of burning

**detention** [dĭ-tĕn´-shən] the act of detaining or holding back

**dilution** [dī-lōō´-shən] something watered down; less concentrated

**a-trice**   Latin — feminine

**cantatrice** [kăn´-tə-trēs] female professional singer

**-tude**   Latin — state, quality, act

**magnitude** [măg´-nĭ-tüd] greatness of size, volume, or extent

**i-tude**   Latin — state, quality, act

**fortitude** [fôr´-tĭ-tüd] courage and strength in bearing pain or trouble

**-ulous**   Latin — having the quality of

**pendulous** [pĕn-jōō´-ləs] hanging loosely or swinging freely

**em-um**   Latin — of or belonging to

**chrysanthemum** [krĭ-săn´-thə-məm] any of a large group of plants with bright yellow, red, or white showy flowers that bloom in late summer or fall

**ult-uous**   Latin — having the quality of

**tumultuous** [tə-mul´-chŏŏ-əs] full of commotion and uproar

**it-ur**   Latin — that which

**non sequitur** [nŏn´-sĕk-wĭ-tōŏr] a remark having no bearing on what has just been said

**-ure**   Latin — state, quality, act; process, condition

**cincture** [sĭnct´-yər] anything that encircles, such as as a belt or girdle

**tenure** [tĕn´-yər] the term during which some position is held

**-us**   Latin — thing which

**Eoanthropus** [ē-ō-an´-thrō-pəs] a genus of early man comprising only the Piltdown man; dawn man

**esophagus** [ĭ-sŏf´-ə-gəs] the part of the digestive tract that connects the throat to the stomach (Medical)

**eucalyptus** [yōō-kə-lĭp´-təs] Australian evergreen tree with rigid leaves and protected flowers and having medicinal and industrial value

**helianthus** [hē-lē-an´-thəs] tall yellow-flowered perennial related to the sunflower

**sarcophagus** [sär-kŏf´-ə-gəs] an ornamental stone coffin used to decompose the flesh of the corpse within

**-y**   Greek — state of, quality, act; body, group

**agony** [āg´-ə-nē] an intense feeling of suffering

**amnesty** [ăm´-nĭ-stē] pardon; literally "forgetting a crime"

**anthography** [ăn-thŏg´-rə-fē] description of flowers

**atrophy** [ă´-trə-fē] to waste away or to decrease in size as of a body part or tissue

**cinematography** [sĭn-ə-mə-tŏg´-rə-fē] the art and methods of photography used in film making

**cryoscopy** [krī-ŏs´-kə-pē] the science dealing with the determination of the freezing points of liquids

**cryotherapy** [krī-ō-thĕr´-ə-pē] therapeutic use of cold

**dactyloscopy** [dăk-tə-lŏ´-skə-pē] examination of fingerprints for purposes of identification

**dystrophy** [dĭs´-trŏ-fē] any degenerative disorder resulting from inadequate or faulty nutrition

**ecstasy** [ĕk´-stə-sē] a state beyond reason and self-control; overwhelming emotion

**hierarchy** [hī´-ə-rär-kē] a system in which people or things are arranged according to their rank or status

**hierocracy** [hī´-ə-rŏk-rə-sē] government by clergymen

**hypertrophy** [hī-pûr´-trə-fē] excessive growth or enlargement of a body part or organ

**hypnotherapy** [hĭp´-nō-thĕr-ə-pē] the use of hypnosis in treating illness or emotional problems

**lithography** [lĭ-thŏg´-rə-fē] the process or method of printing from a metal or stone surface

**melancholy** [mĕl´-ən-kŏl-ē] characterized by or expressing sadness; gloomy

**metallurgy** [mĕt´-l-ûr-jē] the science and technology of extracting metals from their ores

**narcolepsy** [när-kō-lĕp´-sē] a sleep disorder characterized by sudden and uncontrollable episodes of deep sleep

**orthography** [ôr-thŏg´-rə-fē] spelling in accord with accepted usage

**phytotherapy** [fī-tō-thər´-ə-pē] the use of herbs and other plants to promote health and treat disease

**pyretotherapy** [pīr-ĭ-tō-thĕr´-ə-pē] fever therapy

**pyrometallurgy** [pī-rō-mĕt´-l-ûr-jē] chemical metallurgy that depends on heat action

**tachygraphy** [tă-kĭg´-rə-fē] the art or technique of rapid writing or shorthand

**xerography** [zĭ-rŏg´-rə-fē] method of dry photocopying in which the image is transferred by using the forces of electric charges

**xerophagy** [zĭ-rof´-ə-je] eating of dry food